# Crown Princess

A BIOGRAPHY OF DIANA

# Crown
# Princess

## Josephine Fairley

920111

ST. MARTIN'S PRESS NEW YORK

CROWN PRINCESS: A BIOGRAPHY OF DIANA. Copyright © 1992 by
Josephine Fairley. All rights reserved. Printed in the United States
of America. No part of this book may be used or reproduced in
any manner whatsoever without written permission except in the
case of brief quotations embodied in critical articles or reviews.
For information, address St. Martin's Press, 175 Fifth Avenue,
New York, N.Y. 10010.

*Design by Judith A. Stagnitto*

Library of Congress Cataloging-in-Publication Data

Fairley, Josephine.
    Crown Princess : a biography of Diana / Josephine Fairley.
        p.   cm.
    "A Thomas Dunne book."
    ISBN 0-312-07688-6
    Diana, Princess of Wales, 1961-      . 2. Great Britain—
Princes and princesses—Biography.   I. Title.
DA591.A45F35   1992
941.085'092—dc20
[B]

First Edition: August 1992                              92-3149
                                                           CIP

10   9   8   7   6   5   4   3   2   1

*To my father, Peter Fairley, with love*

# Contents

# Introduction

The world's most fa-
mous woman has a
double life.
There is the dazzling existence she leads in public—
always smiling, oh-so-natural, amazingly approachable.
And her secret life, in which she tries—tries *so* hard—
to behave like a normal wife, a normal mother, a normal
friend. Those two sides of the Princess of Wales are
equally fascinating, equally bizarre. For the simple truth
is, Diana can never be normal. Fate has made her a quite
extraordinary woman.

But what is truly, eternally fascinating, is her ability
to change all the time, to reinvent herself constantly.
She's gone from Shy Di to Shopaholic Di, from Disco Di
to Caring Diana, her current incarnation, the crown
princess who has oceans of time for small children, AIDS
patients, and old people, and is throwing herself into
that role with unprecedented passion. It is a passion that,
some say, should be reserved for—and reciprocated

by—the man who chose her as his bride over a decade ago.

Unlike Charles, Diana isn't simply biding her time or twiddling her manicured fingers until the coronation, when she will publicly pledge her allegiance to her country and to her husband forever. Whereas the Prince of Wales seems to grow increasingly impatient with life—searching constantly for meaning, for ways to keep his mind off the fact that he's "just" a king-in-waiting—Diana has vowed that life is for living, *now*. Even if it hasn't turned out quite the way she planned it, all those years ago when (as a teenager) she set her heart on winning a prince's heart.

Diana is living proof that we should all believe in fairy tales—as long as we don't expect them always to have that promised happy ending, with the Prince and the Princess walking off into the sunset, hand in hand. Real life isn't like that, as Diana and Charles have discovered, sometimes to their delight, often to their disappointment. In some ways, the couple has more freedom than any royal couple before them: Diana, for instance, can shop for herself, pick her sons up from school, even drive herself, all of which were unheard of for previous generations of royalty.

At the same time, life has never been more stressful for the Royal Family—and never more public. They've never been expected to work so hard. And Diana and Charles's partnership, like most modern marriages, has been fraught with difficulties. Which of *us* would jump at the prospect of building a relationship in the glare of the spotlight, living in a fishbowl with dozens of lenses trained upon our every move? Diana has been known to wail to friends: "Why can't they leave us alone?" But the public has come to expect access to individuals in the Royal Family in just the same way they can visit the Crown Jewels, or take photos of the Changing of the Guard at Buckingham Palace. The miracle is that so far neither Diana, nor Charles, nor their marriage has cracked under the strain.

Not so long ago, after Prince Charles broke his arm in a horrific polo accident and was out of action for months, a stranger asked Diana if she was going to make him stop playing the dangerous sport he so loves. "No," responded the princess. "You must never stop a man doing what he wants to do." And although she has gently molded her man, improving his dress sense, making him lighten up with her occasional reprimands ("Don't be so stuffy, Charles") the Prince of Wales is still stubbornly the man she married.

The Prince of Wales, however, must sometimes feel as if he's married a stranger. Nobody could have predicted that quiet, timid Diana would blossom into such a beauty, such a hard worker, such a great mom, a woman so at ease in any social situation. (The transformation was so dramatic that in court circles, she was known for a while as "the mouse that roared.") It cannot have been easy for a man so used to being the center of attention to be eclipsed by a young upstart of a girl.

But in fact, Diana is the best news the British monachy has had for years. Occasionally, over the last few years, there have been vague, anarchic rumblings in the United Kingdom that the Royal Family—which is granted massive salaries (in the Queen's case, tax-free) out of taxpayers' money—is a needless extravagance and totally out of date. That the money would be much better spent on health, on education, even on the railways, rather than on buying Fergie another frock or repainting the royal yacht. (Other European countries, after all, have put their royal families out to pasture in this century.)

Diana, though, is the acceptable face of contemporary royalty: the tourist attraction, the international ambassador, the caring workaholic who, when public opinion begins to wobble ever so slightly, gives the royals a valuable boost in opinion polls. She's begun to be likened to the most popular royal of all, Charles's granny the Queen Mother, for her combination of the common touch, regal presence, and sympathy. Her Majesty Queen Elizabeth is thought to look upon her daughter-in-law extremely fondly, knowing that Diana is the perfect queen-in-waiting. And Diana must sometimes feel exasperated that the only man who doesn't seem to recognize her astonishing qualities is Prince Charles himself.

The real stars of the royal show, of course, should by rights be the future kings of England. Really, Diana should be a mere accessory, a loyal wife and mother to Charles and William, those V.V.I.P.s whose faces will one day, fate willing, be on postage stamps and coins. Perhaps that low-key role was even what she wanted for herself—but we weren't going to let it happen. And besides, Diana was simply born to shine. After she'd had a taste of superstardom, the princess began to revel in her new role, deciding to use the public not only to *her* advantage, but for those less well off than she is. This may be some compensation for the way we used *her* and made her our property. She would break with protocol and hug leprosy sufferers and people with AIDS, if that's what she felt like, raising millions for good causes and breaking down public fear into the bargain. She vowed to break the rules and set a new blueprint for working motherhood. And above all, whatever she chose to do, she would do it with that elusive quality: style.

As a result, Diana has become the most popular girl in the world. Bigger than Bardot or the Beatles ever were, more ogled than Jackie O, more loved even than Liz Taylor in her heyday. She is a legend in her own lifetime, rewriting the royal history book. The key is to look behind the scenes—at her family, her friendships, her rivalries, and her luxurious life-style—and try to discover whether Diana, the crown princess, is—after all—destined to have that fairy-tale ending and live happily ever after . . .

# Crown Princess

# 1

# Ten Generations of Royal Groupies

$\mathcal{D}$iana Spencer was born into a family that probably has more royal blood flowing through its veins than Prince Charles's—and almost as much money in the bank. For almost three centuries, the blue-blooded Spencers have been amazingly close to the U.K.'s first family. That long-term friendship has occasionally been touched with scandal. Diana's ancestor Sarah, Duchess of Marlborough (1660–1744) became the wealthiest, most influential woman in England. She was Queen Anne's Lady of the Bedchamber—perhaps in every sense of the word: The two women exchanged passionate love letters. Later on, another ancestor, Lady Georgiana Spencer, stole the heart of King George IV when he was still Prince of Wales—and even though she was married to the Duke of Devonshire at the time, this conspicuous closeness resulted in a flurry of rumors when Georgiana became pregnant.

Two and a half centuries ago, Diana's namesake—an earlier Lady Diana Spencer—was earmarked for

Charles's ancestor, another Prince of Wales, until Britain's prime minister (who had some say in the matter) stepped in and forbade the match. Diana's own grandmother Cynthia was courted by yet *another* Prince of Wales (the same one who abdicated over his love affair with Wallis Simpson). But it wasn't until *this* Diana appeared on the scene that a Spencer finally won the grand prize in the most-eligible-bachelor lottery.

A cynic once referred to the Spencers as "ten generations of royal groupies." Certainly few families have been closer to the royals than the Spencers have—and in exchange they've been rewarded with coveted roles in the royal household: Cynthia was also the Queen Mother's Lady of the Bedchamber (an entirely innocent posting, in this instance) and Diana's own dad, Johnny, has been equerry to both King George VI and Queen Elizabeth. He even once dated her sister, Margaret. What this did for Diana was ensure that, unlike most people, Diana was entirely at ease around royalty, whose company she'd enjoyed almost since the day she was born. And that quality meant a lot to her future husband, who had encountered more than his fair share of awestruck bimbos and social climbers.

Diana learned early, though, that money can't buy happiness. Certainly, she was born into a life of privilege. Her father was the dashing Viscount Althorp (pronounced "Alltrup" by the aristocracy), her mother the stunningly beautiful Lady Frances Fermoy. They lived together in Park House, a beautiful country home in Norfolk, filled with antiques and priceless portraits of fabled ancestors, boasting six live-in staff and a full-time gourmet cook. Johnny, then thirty-two and one of Britain's most eligible bachelors, had swept the tall, blond, slender Frances off her feet, even though he was engaged to another woman at the time. Their high-society nuptials were labeled the wedding of the year—and the finishing touches to the affair seemed to have been added when their first daughter, Sarah, was born just nine months after the big day.

But by the time Diana Spencer—the third daughter (after Sarah and Jane)—made her debut in the world, on July 1, 1961, romance had died and the gulf between Johnny and Frances widened. (Diana was only upgraded to the title of "Lady," incidentally, when her father inherited the earldom on the death of his father in 1975.) Living with in-laws (as many couples discover at a cost) had proved difficult; there had been squabbles over where to move after living with Johnny's irritable papa (then Earl Spencer) had failed. Only when Frances's father died were they able to set up in a home of their own: Her widowed mother kindly offered them the ten-bedroom Park House on the royal Sandringham estate (just a stone's throw, in fact, from where Diana's future husband regularly spent an extended post-Christmas Royal Family break). The couple endured their fair share of tragedy, too. All aristocratic families have a pressing need to produce a male heir (who will inherit all titles and much of the family's wealth); before Diana arrived, Frances had given birth to a son, but he lived only ten hours. Frances's natural sadness at this loss was compounded by a crushing sense of failure.

If she felt any frustration at giving birth to a third healthy girl, however, Lady Althorp disguised it well—and Diana's sisters were certainly thrilled, treating the new baby exactly like a living doll, dressing her in tiny clothes and brushing her hair. And although by now the age gap was yawning between Frances and her husband—fourteen years older, Johnny was putting on weight and sliding rapidly into complacent middle age, content to farm his cattle and be a homebody—she stuck it out until a son, Charles, finally arrived, in May 1964.

On the surface, Diana's childhood was idyllic. Park House was just miles from the beach, perfect for frequent picnic outings. There were ponies and an entire menagerie of pets—and royals—to play with; the young Windsors would invite the young Spencers for tea, cakes, and games, and the Queen took a keen interest in their development, often stopping to chat as she rode through the grounds. In fact, the Spencers were a boisterous lot, testing the patience of an ever-changing cast of nannies, until iron-willed Nanny Thompson arrived and got the better of them. She recalls the young Diana only too well. "She wasn't easy. Some children will do as they're told immediately. Diana wouldn't. It was always a battle of wills." Diana particularly hated going for walks or pony rides or having her long blond hair washed—and as a result was often sent to her room in punishment. She was so aloof at times that the staff nicknamed her "Duchess."

Young Diana's parents lavished love on their children—but apparently not on each other. Her innocent childhood came to an abrupt end. First Diana's beloved elder sisters were sent to West Heath Boarding School. (When Diana was thirteen, she joined them there.) Then came the real bombshell: the departure of Diana's mother.

Girls are always counseled not to marry young; Frances proved the wisdom of that advice, growing up and away from her husband, falling into the arms of another man. At a crowded dinner table she met Peter Shand Kydd, a charming, wealthy, extremely witty man who was married and had three young children of his own. The forbidden affair was both thrilling and heart-breaking. But in Peter's company Frances found the excitement that had gone from her own marriage. Most important, he made her laugh again—and as any woman knows, there's nothing more irresistible. The romance blossomed during a skiing holiday shared by the two families, and upon her return, Lady Althorp arranged a trial separation from Johnny, who was deeply shocked by his wife's decision to leave him. It almost broke her heart to have to explain the facts to her children. The plan was that the four young Spencers would stay with their father only until Frances found a suitable new home. She would almost certainly have thought twice about leaving them if she'd known that she would never live with them again.

Frances moved to London, back into a sophisticated social circle. For a while, Diana and her little brother joined her. Then there was a brief stab at a marital reunion, for one strained Christmas holiday. But it was too late, and the couple felt their only option was to divorce. Only Frances and Johnny know what was said behind closed doors—and neither has ever spilled the beans—but the result was that in late 1968 Frances filed for divorce, citing her husband's cruelty as grounds. She fully expected to get custody of her beloved quartet.

Perhaps she had underestimated Johnny, however. He had his heart set on custody, too—and used every ounce of energy, wielded every bit of power he had, to ensure he got it. He called in favors until, one by one, the couple's friends (and even Frances's mother, Lady Fermoy, herself) were enlisted to speak out against Frances. When the divorce was ultimately granted, the grounds were Frances's adultery with Peter Shand Kydd—and she was not only denied custody, but marked out as something of a scarlet woman. Doors that had been open to her during her marriage to Johnny were slammed in her face, even though her mother was lady-in-waiting to the Queen Mother. As one insider explains, "Frances was completely cut off from everyone." She had to learn to live with the shame of being labeled a bolter, as the upper classes call women who've abandoned duty, husband, or kids.

It is hardly surprising that Frances's second wedding was a low-key event, tinged with sadness and touched by scandal. But the Shand Kydds were for many years extremely happy, splitting their time between two continents. (They had homes in the U.K. and Australia; Diana later visited the latter to seek her mother's advice after she accepted Prince Charles's proposal.) Peter had been described as "a bit of a gypsy, never happy in one place for long, dabbling in different adventures." Sadly that marriage too has floundered, and Frances is alone again. But the Spencer children seem never to have blamed their mother for an event that blighted their childhood; they are all utterly devoted to her. Perhaps, too, Frances is consoled by her social life—for, now that she's single again, the doors that slammed shut after her divorce have reopened.

As all children do, Diana suffered greatly over her parents' divorce. She decided at an early age that she would never put her own children through such torment—and that's one reason she hasn't opted out of her royal marriage, even when the going has seemed particularly tough. Allegedly, she told another nanny, Mary Clarke, "I'll never never ever marry unless I really love someone. If you're not really sure you love someone, then you might get divorced. I never want to be divorced!"

Diana got to visit with her mother during school holidays, staying with the Shand Kydds at their cozy farmhouse in Sussex. Parting after these visits was always painful. But, despite her mother's absence from Park House, life went on—and there was soon the distraction of full-time school. Although aristocratic children are often educated at home, by governesses, Diana and Charles were enrolled in a small local day school, the Silfield School.

Diana was never destined to be a great scholar, however; as a result, she's often been on the receiving end of cracks about her lack of academic qualifications. In fact, she's been known to make a few jokes at her own expense; Prince Charles was once heard warning his wife to mind her head, lest she knock it on a low beam, whereupon she retorted, "Why? There's nothing in it!" But Diana is anything but a dumb blonde. She was simply smart enough to realize that as an eligible, aristocratic young woman, she didn't need a string of certificates and scholarly honors.

Probably as a result of the bitter divorce, Diana had become shy and pensive, playing with her teddy bear in the nursery rather than mixing with other children. So, when she was just eight, her father decided to send her to boarding school. To wrench a child from its parents— or even *parent*—at such an early age may seem alien to Americans, but among the British upper classes it's common practice. In fact, now that he was a bachelor again, Johnny was much in demand socially and could no longer guarantee to be at home on weekends or for nursery visits during the evenings. So Diana—and her favorite guinea pig, Peanuts—were sent off to Riddlesworth, a friendly school less than two hours' drive from her father's home.

To her parents' relief, shy Di bloomed in this cozy, low-pressure environment. She forged friendships with other animal-loving girls and they would spend hours together, tending their furry friends in the school's Pets Corner. (One of Diana's only accolades during her academic years was to win the school's "Pets Corner Cup"; she recalls that she even trained Peanuts to follow her!) Frances and Johnny organized a visiting schedule, bringing her favorite treats of Twiglets (savory biscuits), chocolate cream eggs, and ginger cookies. In turn, she wrote loving weekly letters home, often enclosing drawings dedicated "to Mummy," or "to Daddy," yet somehow forgetting to include news of her occasional pranks, such as writing her name in pencil on the school walls. Diana admits that she was "really naughty" during her stint at Riddlesworth. While paying a return visit there to open a new pre-preparatory building, she confessed to a current pupil: "We used to jump all over the beds, and there was one girl who used to wet her bed—so it was called the water jump!"

Some of Diana's teachers remember her only as being "extremely average." But if she wasn't a brain, she did have other assets. Her former headmistress, Jean Lowe, recalled the school's most famous "old girl" in a school-magazine tribute that declared, "The things that stand out in my memories are her kindness to the smaller members of the community, her general helpfulness, her love of animals, her excellence in swimming, and indeed her considerable prowess in general physical activities." In fact, at Riddlesworth Diana found a security that was lacking at home. Some children are desperately lonely at boarding school, but Diana actually found the routine, the rules, and the strict order comforting.

Before she could join her sisters at West Heath, Diana

had to knuckle down to some hard work in order to pass the crucial Common Entrance examination. To her great relief, she succeeded; she was overjoyed at being in her sisters' company once again. At West Heath, Diana was a model, if undistinguished, pupil. Meanwhile, although big sister Jane was quiet and hardworking, for a time it looked as if fiery redhead Sarah, the eldest Spencer girl, might go off the rails entirely. Although now a firm teetotaler, she wasn't above sneaking a drink during school. "I used to drink because I was bored," Sarah—now Lady Sarah McCorquodale—recalls. "I would drink anything. Whisky, Cointreau, sherry—or, most often, vodka, because they couldn't smell it on my breath." Eventually, her teachers had enough, and wild child Sarah was expelled.

Diana loved sports, playing tennis and swimming competitively. She also showed early signs of a caring nature; at West Heath, there was an emphasis on developing "character and confidence," and girls were encouraged to do community work. For Diana, that meant visiting an old lady in the nearby town to sit and talk and to run errands. She wasn't so keen on lessons. In fact, like many teenaged girls, Diana lived in a fantasy world most of the time. She would bury her nose in the latest sloppily romantic novel by Barbara Cartland (who, ironically, later became Diana's stepgrandmother, when her father married Miss Cartland's daughter Raine). And on her wall in the dormitory (better known as a "cow shed") was a pinup of none other than Prince Charles; insiders suggest that she had earmarked him for herself even at that tender age.

She was still naughty occasionally, as she publicly admitted on an official trip to open a gymnasium dedicated to her retiring former headmistress, Ruth Rudge. After a giggly tour of the school with her two sisters and lady-in-waiting, Anne Beckwith Smith (another West Heath alum), Diana gave a speech to declare the gym open. "Perhaps now, when future generations are handed out for talking after 'lights' [the moment of curfew when dormitory lights must be switched off, or else], pillow fights, and illegal food, they will be told to run six times around this hall. It has to be preferable to weeding the garden, which I became expert at!"

There were few clues, during Diana's time, that she would ever be invited back in such a distinguished role. Her only honor was to scoop the Miss Clark Lawrence Award "for anyone who has done things that might otherwise go unsung." Ruth Rudge remembers her "telling me that winning it was one of the most surprising things that had ever happened to her." Diana still has fond memories of the school. On that outing with her sisters to visit their alma mater, she also recalled, somewhat shamefacedly, "I made many friends whom I often see—and, in spite of what Miss Rudge and my other teachers may have thought, I did actually learn something. Though you wouldn't have thought so from my 'O' Level results!" Diana was referring to her failure to pass even *one* "O" Level, an exam all British sixteen-year-olds take. It isn't uncommon for bright girls to get twelve "O" 's under their belt—yet Diana took hers *twice* and failed to pass in a single subject.

Diana most enjoyed the school holidays, when she could spend chunks of time with her father and mother. When Diana was fifteen, her father was remarried, to the then Lady Dartmouth, Raine, who sometimes has to endure the cruel nickname "Acid Raine." Raine "bolted" from her husband for Johnny, and at first, relations between the Spencer children and their new stepmother were decidedly frosty. The Spencer girls would sing together, "Raine, Raine, go away." Lady Spencer recalls, "Sarah resented me; Jane didn't speak to me for two years, even if we bumped into each other in the passageway. It was bloody awful." But for Johnny, this was a true love match. He explained, "It was a case of two very lonely people who found each other and found happiness together."

The Spencer children warmed to Raine only in the face of near tragedy. In 1978, Johnny Spencer suffered a stroke and lapsed into a coma. He almost died. Not for a moment did his wife leave his bedside, and her affection and devotion finally won her stepchildren's affection. As Johnny recalled, "Raine saved my life. Without Raine I would never have lived to see Diana married, never mind walking up the aisle of St. Paul's." (Those who were watching may remember his slight limp.) "Raine sat with me for four solid months, holding my hand and even shouting at me that I wasn't going to die because she wasn't going to let me." The Wicked Stepmother was no more.

When Diana left school at sixteen, college was out of the question. The only hope now was to polish her in the hope that she might make a fine marriage; she joined a band of young aristocrats at an expensive Swiss finishing school in the Alps, the Institut Alpin Videmanette, to learn French, secretarial skills, and cooking. But it was a disaster; Diana understood little of what she was being taught (lessons were conducted in French, and hers was anything but fluent), and she has always been prone to crushing homesickness. So she returned to the fold, only a little older—and certainly not much wiser.

Meanwhile, there was great excitement in the Spencer household. Diana's older sister Sarah was dating Prince

Charles—and being touted as a potential bride. In January 1978, after being escorted by Charles and gossiped about as his favorite girlfriend, she accompanied him on a skiing holiday to Klosters, Switzerland. Sarah gloried in the media attention and adored having her picture taken. She even took out a subscription to a clipping service so she wouldn't miss a single mention of her name in the newspapers.

But Sarah eventualy spoiled her chance to be a royal bride by breaking a taboo: she talked to the press about her relationship with Prince Charles. "He is a fabulous person, but I am not in love with him," she explained. He was like the big brother she'd never had, she insisted, and there were other fish in the sea. "I wouldn't marry anyone I didn't love—whether it was the dustman or the King of England. If he asked me, I would turn him down." By speaking out, however, she guaranteed that whatever the state of Charles's feelings, a proposal definitely wasn't in the cards.

It's said, though, that the young Diana was green with envy over her sister dating her own pinup. "There will always be a jealousy problem between Sarah and the princess," reports an insider, "following Sarah's flirtation with Charles. There is an ever-present edge. That's why Diana was never keen to stay in the same ski chalet that Charles had shared with Sarah." But Sarah is now happily married to a former Coldstream Guards officer, dashing Neil McCorquodale, and has two children, Emily Jane and George. And relations between the sisters mellowed around the time Diana dieted herself into excessive slenderness, just before her wedding to Prince Charles. "Don't lose another pound, Di!' screamed the newspaper headlines; and Sarah was able to offer insights into the dieter's disease anorexia nervosa, because she, too, had suffered from it while dating Charles. (Seems that going steady with a prince is enough to put a girl off her food.) At the height of her illness, Sarah slimmed down from a shapely 34-24-34 to a skeletal 27-20-28. Insiders say Charles was, in fact, Sarah's salvation; it's known that almost as soon as the two began dating, he boldly asked out loud if she was anorexic—and perhaps it's no coincidence that just a couple of months later, she went into the hospital for treatment and slowly began to build her appetite.

Diana is still much closer, though, to her other sister, Jane; in fact, the two are neighbors. Jane's husband Robert Fellowes has long been the queen's deputy private secretary, and a perk of the post is "grace and favor" apartments in opulent Kensington Palace—just across the courtyard from Diana; the Fellowes children, Laura, Alexander, and Eleanor, are playmates of the young princes, and Diana has a teasing, close relationship with Jane's Old Etonian husband, Robert.

Jane was the complete opposite of rebel Sarah. Declares a friend, "Jane did everything by the book—but that doesn't mean she was boring. She just knew what she wanted. Jane is not as physically attractive as her two sisters, but she has a great sense of fun when off duty." She was certainly more of a bookworm than Diana: She passed eleven "O" Levels. Jane, who had worked as an editorial assistant at *Vogue* magazine, actually played fairy godmother during Diana's romance by introducing her to style experts at the magazine who helped transform the ingenue into a true princess of style. Jane is known for her cool head. In fact, at the time of the royal engagement, it was she who sounded a lone warning note in all the euphoria; she was overheard saying, "Diana doesn't know what she's letting herself in for."

It is Diana's younger brother, Charles, who has brought fresh scandal to this new generation of Spencers. Tall, redheaded, and handsome, Charles—Viscount Althorp—was one of Britain's most eligible young bachelors, working as a reporter for the NBC network in London; he had thrown off an early reputation as "Champagne Charlie," with a taste for the high life, and was devoting himself to his TV career. Then along came wide-eyed, brunette model Victoria Lockwood; the two enjoyed a whirlwind romance and within six weeks, announced their engagement. Extravagant nuptials were planned at the church of St. Mary-the-Virgin between the Princess of Wales's brother and twenty-four-year-old Miss Nobody (the daughter of a Civil Aviation Authority executive) from Barnes, in South-West London. She glided down the aisle a mere commoner, and emerged from the church an aristocrat, the new Viscountess Althorp, the next Countess Spencer—and was immediately admitted to an exclusive but growing circle: the nearly royals. One of her pageboys was Prince Harry, wearing a flouncy pastoral costume he will probably cringe over in later years; there's a photograph of a glum-looking Harry proudly displayed in the hallway at Highgrove, Diana and Charles's country estate.

But, on what should have been the happiest day of her life, this bride looked as miserable as the weather. Perhaps she was upset by a newspaper report about an ex-boyfriend who had turned out to be a heroin addict. She came in for a lot of criticism over her fur-trimmed Tomas Starzewski dress, too; some reports suggested it looked as if it had been run up from a pair of old cream brocade curtains. Worse, it wasn't many months before a question mark hung over the couple's happiness. They were rarely seen in public together; rumors of arguments seeped out. Then Victoria got pregnant, and it seemed the couple's whirlwind romance would have a happy ending after all when their daughter, Kitty Eleanor, was born.

Then came the fireworks: Just weeks after Kitty's birth, Viscount Althorp took the unprecedented step of going public about an adulterous fling, confessing to the *Daily Mail*'s gossip guru, Nigel Dempster, that he'd had a one-night stand with journalist and cartoonist Sally Ann Lasson. The world was aghast. Two days later, Charles's reasons became clear: Sally Ann had decided to "kiss and sell" the lurid details of their liaison to the tabloids, grabbing front-page headlines.

I had always thought Sally Ann to be utterly discreet; in fact, she is a friend of a friend, and I used to go with her to visit a mutual acquaintance, who had been hospitalized after a stroke. Around the bedside, girls' gossip continued as usual, with our recovering friend listening raptly while Sally Ann revealed the gripping ups and downs of her relationship with An Unnamed Man. No matter what we did, we couldn't persuade her to spill the beans about his identity. Imagine my surprise, then, when it turned out to be Viscount Althorp.

From Sally Ann's account at that time, the fatal attraction was far more than a one-night stand. But Charles admitted only to the following: that six months after his wedding, when going through an "extremely unpleasant patch" in his marriage, he had a one-night stand with Sally Ann, the result of a "particularly unpleasant series of quarrels" with his wife. At that time, he insisted, he had believed that any chance of a reconciliation was out of the question.

By gossip standards, the story was Grade A juicy. Sally

Ann appeared the typical woman scorned, branding Charles "a cad" who "used her"—and, having broken a high-society rule never to kiss and sell, found herself dropped by her upmarket friends and even her employers; *Tatler* magazine, the "top" people's glossy monthly, immediately dropped her column. It does seem particularly cruel to have chosen to reveal all just a few weeks after the birth of an innocent child—and if she did it for money, the plan backfired; rumor has it that she earned $100,000 for her story but may well have lost that much in potential income from more respectable sources.

But people began to ask the question: Did Diana's brother make a terrible error of judgment in coming clean? Without his confirmation of the lurid tale, libel lawyers might have felt too anxious abut possible repercussions of Sally Ann's lurid story to run with it. But in fact, Charles has never been publicity-shy and seems to relish basking in the limelight. Another friend tells me that he gladly gossiped with her about all sorts of quite intimate details of his royal sister's life—and *she* believes that he may have been the source of several newspaper stories about Diana. (Another insider, meanwhile, says that a lot of the stories actually come from the princess herself, and that she is not above phoning gossip columnists with items of tittle-tattle.)

Victoria was certainly shattered by Charles's revelations, but she was determined to put a brave face on the episode. Charles's statement said that the experience of his one-night stand in Paris with Sally Ann—a few years after their *first* one-night stand—"so sickened me that I did not stay the second night in Paris, but returned to London, eager to patch up my marriage. This my wife and I were able to do to such an extent that today, a month after the birth of our first child, we are deeply in love." *The Sun* newspaper claimed a scoop when Victoria, her voice quivering with emotion, explained on the phone to a reporter that "we are together and will continue to be so." But the marriage was put under further stress a few weeks later, when Charles lost his lucrative job with NBC—allegedly in a bout of cost-cutting. But in fact, his was the *only* position axed.

It must have been a nasty moment for Charles Althorp when he had to ring his sister and explain that she was about to be embarrassed publicly by his dangerous liaison. Diana, in turn, had to inform her mother-in-law, the Queen—but instead of being furious with Charles for dragging the family name through the mud, Diana tried to give him helpful advice that would help the viscount and his viscountess mend their marriage, drawing on her experience as president of the marriage-counseling agency Relate; Althorp called her several times during the debacle and says he will never forget her sound advice and sisterly loyalty.

Earl Spencer was thought to have been distinctly unamused by his son's peccadillo; Diana may well have managed to calm him down, too. Her father, whom she so nearly lost when she was a teenager, was especially precious to her. She was a frequent visitor at the oh-so-grand Spencer House (which the Spencers opened to the public in order to raise money toward the cost of maintaining such a massive monument. "We've got to make this place pay," Lord Spencer would explain, sometimes even serving behind the counter in the stately home's shop. "If that means throwing a party for Tupperware manufacturers, why not?"). Diana spoke to her father several times a week on the phone and was known to drop in unannounced to cook bacon and eggs for him.

But during times of stress during her *own* life, and particularly during her marriage, Diana turned to her mother for solace and advice. Despite the fact that mother and daughter have been separated by miles for much of Diana's adult life, they treasure their time together and have become very close. It was to her mother's Australian ranch that Diana escaped in order to reflect after Prince Charles proposed. And having weathered the storms of a highly publicized divorce from Johnny, Frances was quite the best person to put her daughter back on the straight and narrow during a rocky patch in Diana's marriage when she may have felt the urge to bail out. According to Harold Brooks-Baker, publisher of the upper-crust *Who's Who, Debrett's Peerage,* Frances's advice was a key element in helping Diana to realize that she and Charles "*had* to stick it out and be successful in their marriage."

Down the centuries there has been more than enough sensation in Diana's family: affairs, illegitimate births, bitter divorces. With a little help, support, and advice from her family, Diana is trying to ensure that she doesn't cause the greatest scandal yet to taint the Spencer family name.

# 2

# *What Happens When You Kiss a Prince*

*D*iana was once described to me, by an intimate of the royal circle, as "a sacrificial virgin." Marrying the prince, continued the insider, "was a dirty job—but someone had to do it." Not that my source was implying that there is anything wrong with Prince Charles himself, you understand. It's simply that becoming the wife of the heir to the throne means being subjected to life in a fishbowl, never having any privacy again—and being denied the usual escape route if a marriage flounders: Divorce is just not an option.

But if Diana was a human sacrifice, then she chose that role herself. She dreamed about it night and day. When her contemporaries plastered their walls with pin-ups of actors and rock stars, Diana only had eyes for one man: the future king. And unlike most young women, who never get near enough to their hero even to ask for an autograph or blow a kiss, Diana realized that this man was within her grasp—provided she played her cards right. It's hard to believe, but it's almost as if Diana *kept* herself for him. What other reason, in these permissive days, to hang onto your virginity?

By the time Lady Diana Spencer reached maturity and blossomed into a (pure) young swan, the subject of a future bride for Prince Charles had begun to trouble the queen. He was, without question, the world's most eligible bachelor, even though he'd already begun thinning on top and wasn't exactly competiton for Tom Cruise. He made an unlikely sex symbol, but that didn't keep hundreds of girls from yearning to seduce him. On royal tours, he'd had to put a stop to "walkabouts," because girls would appear from nowhere to plant huge kisses on his lips. Once, in Australia, when he went for an early-morning swim, a bikinied blonde bounded through the surf and quite literally flung herself at him. Such assaults had the prince's detectives in a frenzy over the breaches in security.

He'd had a long string of affairs—some serious, some playful—but none had even come close to ending in matrimony. There was Sabrina Guinness, daughter of a wealthy banking and brewing family—a star-struck creature who ended up nannying for David Bowie instead of marrying a prince. Lady Jane Wellesley, the extremely suitable daughter of the Duke of Wellington, had been an early contender for the role, but the two had drifted apart when Charles took up a naval post at sea; besides, Jane had probably proved herself incapable of standing the heat when she was reduced to tears by teams of paparazzi who trailed her everywhere as soon as news of the royal romance leaked out. Lately, he'd had a painful breakup from the spirited Anna Wallace, known to her intimates as "Whiplash," allegedly because of her love of fox hunting (a passion she shared with the prince). She also had a raucous wit, and Charles has always responded well to people who make him laugh. She's said to be the grand passion of his life.

Anna Wallace didn't come from a particularly suitable background, but Charles was smitten. She was even invited to a royal house party at Balmoral for the monarch's inspection. Allegedly, Charles went so far as to propose to Anna, but she turned him down flat. A willful girl, older than Diana by nearly a decade, perhaps she had some insight into how pressured, how public, how *impossible* life would be if she married Prince Charles. Perhaps she was simply worried that amorous skeletons in her closet might come tumbling out if she agreed to his proposal. Either way, at a party for the Queen Mum's eightieth birthday, she flounced out of Charles's life for good after a blistering row in which she accused him of having ignored her all evening. She left not so much as a glass slipper behind. Later, she intimated to friends that she couldn't face a life of planting trees and shaking hands.

Charles was still licking his wounds when Lady Diana Spencer appeared on the scene, invited by Lady Sarah Armstrong-Jones (Princess Margaret's daughter), to a party aboard the royal yacht *Britannia,* during Cowes Regatta Week. In fact, unbeknownst to either Diana or Charles, the Queen Mother—concerned that her beloved grandson was in danger of sliding into lonely middle age—had begun to draw up a list of potential brides. (It was a very short list, but Diana featured prominently.) Sarah Armstrong-Jones beat matchmaking Grandma to the post. But Charles didn't immediately take the bait. Thirteen years younger than Charles, Diana was almost a generation away from him. He really thought of her just as the younger sister of his old flame Lady Sarah Spencer.

It was Sarah Spencer, in fact, who'd engineered the very first real encounter between Charles and his future bride—in 1977, when Diana was *definitely* too young to catch the prince's eye. Sarah had blown her chances of marrying Charles by telling (almost) all to the press, but the two had always enjoyed each other's company and stayed in contact. So she invited him to a weekend shooting party at Althorp, where Diana and Charles were introduced in a muddy field. Both insist they can't remember—but who can believe Diana? She was already crazy about the prince, and for a bored schoolgirl, an encounter with the man of her dreams would have been a real landmark. It was around that time that Diana jokingly told a friend (or at least, the friend *thought* it was a joke) she was "out to get" Charles.

In the intervening years, meanwhile, Diana blossomed into a beauty—although when she strode up the gangplank of the royal yacht, she was also still a shy, rather plump girl, desperately undereducated. Some call her fresh, some call her innocent, some call her plain naïve. But some elusive quality of hers caught the prince's attention. And when Diana's sister Jane invited her to Balmoral a short while later, to keep her company after the birth of her baby, the prince and the shy girl got to know each other a little better. . . .

If Diana hates Balmoral now, back then she put on a damned good show that she believed it to be paradise. She brought along a piece of dainty needlework to occupy herself while her heartthrob traipsed the stag moors, and she would join in gleefully with charades in the evening. Charles soon found that after a decade of fast women, Diana was like a breath of fresh Highlands air. Meanwhile, Diana was being closely inspected for her suitability—not just by Charles, but by his family. She passed with flying colors, as far as the queen was concerned—Her Majesty having already accepted that a wide age gap between her son and his bride was inevitable.

It does seem strange that the most important qualification for becoming Princess of Wales should have been virginity, but it's true. By 1980, virginity was something most young women were trying desperately to unburden themselves of by the time they reached Diana's age—but that was just too dangerous, as far as the royal family was concerned. They couldn't risk some heartbroken, opportunist boyfriend emerging from the shadows to tell intimate details of his sex life with the future Queen of England to a gossip-hungry world. But in this day and age, that's precisely what would have happened if Charles had settled on a girl with, say, Fergie's woman-of-the-world ways. In Diana's case, there had been only innocent friendships—with Scots Guardsman Rory Scott, who used to wash his shirts in her washing machine, or her occasional dining companions, Old Etonian Simon Berry and gardening expert George Plumptree.

Back in London, at her three-bedroom flat in Coleherne Court—a gift from wealthy Earl Spencer—the coltish, demure Lady Di soon began receiving thrilling phone calls from Buckingham Palace, inviting her to dinner with Charles or to dancing with friends at Annabel's. Occasionally, Diana would return home to find a bouquet of roses waiting for her. Her friends were sworn to secrecy about the identity of the admirer, but Di's roommates, Carolyn Pride, Anne Bolton, and Virginia Pitman, certainly had their fingers crossed.

On the surface, Charles and Diana made an odd couple. She was nearly a generation younger than almost all of his friends, and too shy at that stage to speak except when she was spoken to. She was a high school dropout; he ranks as an intellectual. She doesn't even like horses, which is a fatal flaw in royalty's eyes. Yet somehow, there was an ease in their friendship that he hadn't experienced with any other woman. Perhaps this was because Diana, raised in a family that had been linked to royalty through several centuries, was able to be *herself* around him, totally unawed by his unique status. For Charles, that was a rare treat. And of course, there was her love of children—essential to any future bride, since her main role in life would be to provide him with an heir.

As soon as the press got wind of the romance, Diana's life was transformed forever. She couldn't cross the road for a pint of milk without being photographed. In fact, she secretly reveled in the attention, smiling through the siege. She bought all the newspapers every day and would giggle with her roommates over the day's revelations. She enjoyed the thrill of the chase, too; secret trysts with Charles, even high-speed car dashes, added to the excitement that any woman would experience during her first love affair. For the first time in her life, Diana began to feel beautiful and to take great care with her appearance. When photographers—almost three hundred of them—descended for a photo opportunity at the Young England Nursery School, where Diana helped with the kindergarten kids, was she *really* entirely ignorant of the fact that her translucent skirt, chosen for the occasion, showed off a pair of stunning legs as she stood against the sunlight? I'm not so sure.

Charles rather liked the way his new companion was coming out of her shell. She was a fascinating mixture of fresh and vulnerable, shy and glamorous. And she earned the approval of his closest female friends, Lady "Kanga" Tryon and Lady Camilla Parker-Bowles. When word of the blossoming relationship eventually leaked out, Barbara Cartland, Diana's eternally romantic step-grandmother, declared: "Prince Charles has got to have a pure young girl. I don't think Diana has even had a boyfriend. That is marvelous." Di's uncle, Lord Fermoy (who later, tragically, committed suicide), was quoted as saying, "She, I can assure you, has never had a lover." The press adored her for her constant cooperation and politeness. The royals were beginning to wonder, mean-while, if they hadn't opened a real Pandora's box; no (potential) royal bride had ever commanded so much attention or grabbed so many headlines. When Diana was invited to Sandringham over the Christmas holi-days—and was pursued by an uninvited "rat pack" of reporters—Prince Edward got so mad he fired a gun above their heads. Prince Charles grimly wished their editors "an unhappy New Year."

It may well be that Charles was feeling the intense pressure to make up his mind. Pressure came from all sides, including his mother, who encouraged him to make a decision soon. Everyone was rushing him—ex-cept for the quietly expectant Diana, who was her sweet self, pretending that nothing unusual was happening at all, barely referring to the frenzy of press speculation. Lady Diana—who seemed to grow more beautiful with every photo—had captured the heart of a nation. She confidently expected to do the same with her prince. He had, after all, already given her a privileged guided tour of Highgrove, the place that might be their future home. (Diana was distinctly unimpressed with the dark, somewhat run-down house, but she managed not to let it show).

In fact, on January 14, 1981, a family powwow was called between Lord Spencer and the Queen. The possibility of a royal marriage was at last discussed, and Johnny Spencer left Sandringham a very happy man indeed. Diana had to wait for her *formal* proposal, however, until Charles had returned from his annual skiing jaunt to Klosters. To her disappointment, she'd had to stay home; Charles was worried that, in the Rat Pack's desperation to photograph Diana on the slopes, she might be injured.

When Charles invited her for an intimate dinner in his rooms at Buckingham Palace—where she'd become a regular guest, although she had *certainly* never yet spent a night—Lady Di knew what was in store. She could barely contain her excitement. In the end, he didn't get down on one knee ("not on either of them," he later recalled), but popped the question over a light supper, which Diana barely touched. Diana was due to join her mother in Australia for a holiday, and Charles remembers that "I chose the moment so that she would have plenty of time to think about it, to decide if it wasn't going to be too awful." But nothing was going to put Diana off now that her dream was within reach—and she wasn't going to run the risk that Charles might change her mind while she was Down Under.

Charles had tried to explain to Diana what she might be letting herself in for. But no one could. First, she wouldn't have listened. But second, nobody could have predicted the bad case of Royal Wedding Fever that subsequently broke out. From the moment the engagement was officially announced—on February 24, at eleven A.M., at a photo session on the lawn at Buckingham Palace, with Diana in a cornflower-blue suit that perfectly showed off her diamond-and-sapphire engagement ring—her life was never to be the same again. There were to be many moments when she would yearn for the peace and normality she'd left behind. A notice on the front gates of Buckingham Palace read: "It is with the greatest of pleasure that the Queen and the Duke of Edinburgh announce the betrothal of their beloved son, the Prince of Wales, to Lady Diana Spencer, daughter of the Earl Spencer and the Hon. Mrs. Shand Kydd." The sign made headline news around the world. Dianamania was born.

Like any excited bride-to-be, Diana showed off her ring. She had fallen in love with the diamond-and-sapphire ring the minute she saw it glinting on the black velvet tray with the other rings that Garrards, the crown jewelers, had sent around for the prince and future princess's inspection. "It was the biggest," she said, laughing. "I still can't get used to it." When the waiting reporters asked the prince the obvious question—"Are you in love?"—he replied, "Yes—whatever that means." Nobody needed to ask Diana; the answer was written all over her glowing face. Deftly deflecting questions about the twelve years that separated them, Charles responded, "I have never thought about the age gap. Diana will always keep me young."

Then began the makeover. Like other royal brides before her—the Duchess of Kent, the Duchess of Gloucester (both married to the Queen's cousins)—Diana had every aspect of her life and looks overhauled by palace experts. She was given biographies of royal personalities to read, and that was just the beginning of her homework. She was taught how to do the royal handshake (a light, brief grasp is essential when you have thousands of hands to shake each day), and the discreet royal wave. As a member of the aristocracy, she had impeccable manners, but she had to learn whom to defer to in the royal pecking order, and—perhaps more important—how to deal with the countless lesser mortals who would now be looking up to her; she had to learn not to giggle when every woman in sight dipped into a curtsey when she appeared.

Any spare moments had to be spent writing polite thank-you notes for the extravagant wedding gifts—from heads of state and housewives alike—that were flooding into the palace. (The gifts eventually totaled ten thousand.) She had to learn to live with having a detective following her all the time, even standing guard at the bathroom door! Sometimes, the feeling of being cooped up got to be too much for her. On one occasion, Diana thought she'd pop out for a breath of air. She got into her red Metro car—and found a member of the Royal Protection Squad climbing in beside her. She told him she didn't need him, she'd be fine on her own. "I'm sorry," he told her, "but we're part of your life now." There was to be no more carefree, leisurely browsing in stores.

Diana also had to endure the indignity of a gynecological examination to ensure that she was physically capable of producing an heir for Charles; the experience is known to have left her tearful and feeling vulnerable.

Immediately after the engagement was announced, Diana's possessions at Coleherne Court were packed up; her roommates were told the apartment was to be sold, but not to panic—they'd be given plenty of time to find other homes before being "evicted." It was months before the apartment Diana had been so proud of was put on the market; it sold at a handsome profit, its curiosity value considerably enhanced. The bride-to-be moved into a suite of rooms at Buckingham Palace (the public was led to believe that she'd actually been removed to a more discreet distance from her husband, with his grandmother at Clarence House). According to royal expert and author Ralph Martin, "she lived on the same floor as Charles. He was on one end of the corridor, and she was on the other, with no-one but a few servants in between."

At some point, the two began a physical relationship, which was of great comfort to Diana through the stressful learning period of her engagement. There's nothing like a pair of strong arms around you at night to banish fears and worries. Royal Rat Packer James Whitaker swears that he can pinpoint the evening Diana lost her virginity. The couple were spending a weekend with Andrew's old flame Camilla Parker-Bowles and her husband, also named Andrew. According to Whitaker, "When she emerged next day, she looked quite different—wiser and sexier."

The future king and his future bride were conducting their courtship backwards, in a way. The decision to marry had been made *before* they got to know each other better, rather like the arranged marriages of the East, in fact. Charles and Di found themselves under great pressure; their only peace was at Buckingham Palace. Wherever they stepped outside, flashbulbs started popping—and even close friends excited about the upcoming event asked questions about how the plans were going. They were *the* hot couple to have on your invitation list. Diana was being treated like a star wherever she went. But she had to remember not to act like one. It was a delicate balancing act which, for the most part, she carried off to perfection.

Embarrassed by pictures and television shots of herself looking less than svelte, Diana began to diet, skipping meals whenever she could; as a result, she became quite short-tempered at times. (Besides, she found that she had absolutely no time to herself, which was highly frustrating for a young woman who missed the casual camaraderie of single life, sitting around leafing through the day's papers and sharing high-society gossip with her roommates.) If the public was amazed by the beauty that began to emerge from beneath the layers of puppy fat and unflattering clothing, so was Diana, who had never guessed that she had the potential to become one of the great beauties of her era. But with the help of a new hairstyle (courtesy of Kevin Shanley), advice from top makeup artist Barbara Daly, and an entire wardrobe of clothes selected by experts at *Vogue*, Diana began to look like a contemporary goddess. The pounds were falling off her—to her great delight; she knew only too well that TV gives the illusion that you're ten pounds heavier. Knowing that her wedding would be beamed around the world into billions of living rooms, Diana was determined to have herself a perfect model's figure on her big day.

To make her wedding dress, Diana had selected a young design team that had already created one controversial item for her: a black taffeta evening dress that had been a little *too* revealingly low cut for the Queen's liking. The commission to create the royal wedding dress—an extravagant, pearl-encrusted, cream raw-silk number—was a great break for husband and wife David and Elizabeth Emanuel. But Diana kept needing extra fittings because of her ever-diminishing waistline.

Still, she withstood the strains and stresses of the buildup to the wedding day remarkably well. Her composure cracked only once, at a normally sedate polo match just five days before her wedding; she'd gone to lend her support to Prince Charles. The crowd became distinctly uncivilized, fevered to get a glimpse of the princess-to-be—and almost crushed her in the process. She rushed off in floods of tears and spent a few minutes weeping in the ladies' room; then she removed the mascara streaks, touched up her makeup, and bravely reemerged to face her public.

Diana spent the evening before her wedding quietly at Clarence House, with the Queen Mother. Prince Charles had a stag night, at Julie's Restaurant in Notting Hill Gate, and Diana was a shade disappointed that her former flatmates didn't arrange a bridal shower somewhere. But reporters had been wildly phoning every restaurant in the capital, trying to get a hint of any arrangements, so a party would almost certainly have been ruined.

The day itself dawned bright and clear. Diana was awake long before dawn, trying to quiet the butterflies in her stomach. The morning seemed to pass incredibly slowly; she wolfed down a huge breakfast ("to stop my tummy rumbling in St. Paul's Cathedral") and waited for her usual hairdresser and makeup artist to arrive in time to transform her for this most extraordinary event. Diana had specified that she wanted to look as natural as possible, and Daly and Shanley hardly had to do a thing. Lady Di was positively glowing.

From Clarence House, Diana could hear the shouts of the crowds, who'd slept on the pavement overnight, hysterical for a glimpse of her. When she slipped into her dress, it finally fit like a glove. Recalls the Greek seamstress who had cut and stitched the precious dress, "Lady Diana cried . . . and shivered . . . and there were tears in her eyes." There were tears in her father's eyes, too, when the bride emerged to take his arm for the long journey to St. Paul's. Diana had been desperately worried that the excitement would prove too much for her darling daddy; it was only three years since his terrible cerebral hemorrhage, after all. But on July 29, 1981, the only sign that there was anything at all the matter was the slight limp he showed when walking his daughter slowly up the aisle.

For royal brides, love and marriage go together *in* a horse and carriage: the famous gilded Glass Coach. In fact, the designers of the wedding dress hadn't quite realized what the cramped coach would do to their dress, crumpling its twenty-five-foot train like tissue paper, so that when Diana stepped down after her two-mile journey, it emerged creased—and was much criticized. With final tweaks from the Emanuels, who had been hiding in the doorway of the magnificent Christopher Wren–designed cathedral, wanting to make their last-minute adjustments, Diana was ready for the longest walk of her life.

To the great relief of guests, who'd been fidgeting in their places for an hour and a half, the ceremony began, with massed trumpets heralding the bride's arrival. She glided slowly, taking a full three and a half minutes to reach her groom. Afterward Diana admitted, "I was so nervous I hardly knew what I was doing." The nerves showed, too: in front of 700 million viewers, and a cathedral full of dignitaries from crowned heads to Nancy Reagan, she muddled the order of her husband's names.

During the service, nobody failed to note that her wedding vows did *not* include the word "obey"—and that, by some slip of the tongue, Charles had managed *not* to agree to share all his worldly goods with his bride! Apparently, Princess Anne insisted afterward that he'd meant it.

But the ring of Welsh gold was slipped onto the bride's finger. Prince Charles whispered to his bride, "We are married at last," and in spite of her beating heart she managed a shy smile. The full weight of the occasion, of what she had let herself in for, had really hit her— perhaps for the first time. Inside St. Paul's Cathedral, the real transformation of Lady Diana Spencer had taken place. The blushing bride went inside to greet her husband with her head shyly bowed. She emerged with it held high. Shy Di was banished into the history books. Diana, the so-regal Princess of Wales, took her place.

# 3

# Playing Happy Royal Families

hen Diana married Charles she hitched herself to her husband's entire family. The Royal Family is closer than most and grabs frequent opportunities to spend spare time together. Christmas, Easter, Ascot Week, and long summer breaks are fixtures in the royal calendar; whether she likes it or not, Diana's name features prominently on the guest list. As a result, from the day of her betrothal onward, she hasn't been able to enjoy as much time as she'd like in the bosom of her *own* family.

Diana would love to have spent Christmas with her father occasionally. She is said to have been so homesick during one early royal Yule that she fled to her room in floods of tears. She also longs to play hostess *herself*. But instead, Diana must join her husband's family at Windsor or (during the mega renovations at that castle) at Sandringham, which is close enough to Diana's former home at Park House for the occasional nostalgic stroll to bring back sweet memories). But even though Johnny

Spencer is an old friend of the Queen's, and Diana's grandmother is the Queen Mother's best friend, in-laws are simply never invited. Diana must make do with a brief early-December visit to her father: The earl hosts a lavish children's party for his grandchildren with Jell-O and soda, and a magician who later dresses up as Santa Claus.

Sandringham, in an idyllic country setting perfect for the traditional English Christmas, always used to be the Queen's preferred choice for Christmas. But as her family grew larger, bringing with them an ever-widening retinue of nannies, dressers, valets, and minders, Windsor was chosen for practical reasons—it has literally hundreds of rooms—although guests complain that, like Sandringham, it's on the chilly side.

The royals love the intimacy of Sandringham (though intimacy is relative; once upon a time, there was a room for each day of the year, until the ever-thrifty Elizabeth had several wings demolished in 1971). As a result of Windsor Castle's protracted renovations, the Queen's invitation list has been slashed to just the closest relations, who now, of course, include Diana. The honored guests arrive, usually on the day before Christmas Eve, and while their luggage is being collected by the "coal-men" (the title given to a particular rank of servants), members of the family go off to meet "Granny"—aka H.M. the Queen. They bow or curtsey to the monarch even on this most intimate of occasions. (In fact, like all women in the royal household, Diana must curtsey to the Queen every time she sees her; she has likened this to standing on a moving carpet, as the Queen's yapping corgis swarm around her feet.) This formality has been known to drive guests into a nervous frenzy; all royal ladies must be curtseyed to, first encounter of the day and last at night. Declares a royal friend: "You spend the whole morning waiting for them to appear round the corner so you can curtsey and forget about it." In addition, you do not rise before the Queen rises, you do not sit until she sits, and you do not go to bed before H.M. retires, even if you're crying with fatigue. (It's said, though, that the boisterous Duchess of York has taken some of the stiffness and stuffiness out of Christmas in a way that shyer Diana never achieved.)

The house is already decked with holly, ivy, and mistletoe fetched by the Queen, her mother, and Princess Margaret from around the grounds. The place is made to look even more homey by strategic piles of the latest glossy fashion and country life-style magazines and dozens of porcelain cachepots filled with poinsettias and cyclamens from the Queen's own hothouses. The family congregates around a roaring log fire in the living room, a room filled with comfortable sofas to sink into after a long lunch. There's a grand piano in the corner, and Diana and Princess Margaret take turns entertaining the guests; Diana plays everything from Chopin to Mozart, with a little Cole Porter thrown in, while Margaret's renowned for her bluesy recitals and, on occasion, outrageously raucous after-dinner sing-alongs. So far, neither Prince William nor Harry has taken to the keyboard. But they quietly take up their places underneath the piano when their mother is playing, to hear better. Charles is also a fan of his wife's music, but prefers the more formal vantage point of the sofa.

Every bedroom is extremely cozy: bottles of Malvern water on the bedside table, fresh flowers, and a small dish of chocolates for late-night snacking. On the desk, there's engraved writing paper (great for impressing your friends), a letter opener, pens, pencils, even a ball of string. Nothing is forgotten, and the Queen will have checked each room personally. The chimneys were all blocked up years ago, though, so the rooms instead boast electric fires to fend off the chill winds, which come straight off the North Sea and seem to blast straight through the window frames. Attention to detail is fanatical, and there are always servants on hand; the family gets on with enjoying itself while clothes are pressed and hung up. Even toothbrushes are laid out in the private bathrooms.

The Windsors do their gift-giving on Christmas Eve rather than Christmas Day, a tradition handed down from Danish Queen Alexandra, a royal ancestor. There are simply too many gifts to put under even the royals' huge, decorated tree—that's reserved for the children's surprises—so the staff arrange the adults' booty on damask cloths covering trestle tables down one side of the living room. Tea is served, and then the staff gracefully retire so the fun can truly commence. With billions in the bank, the royals could afford to splurge on exotic, extravagant presents—cars, fur coats, priceless jewels. But, despite being surrounded by luxury, they hate ostentation in gifts; it's rare for anyone to get an expensive piece of silver or a jewel. Diana knows not to expect a glittering bauble from her husband. Once, while checking one jeweler's artistic creations, Charles inquired about the price. "Nine thousand pounds? That's far too expensive," responded the multimillionaire prince.

Buying presents for each other must, in fact, be a nightmare—what on earth should Diana get for her mother-in-law, for instance, a woman who really *does* have everything? Perhaps the royals have gotten into the habit of giving small, fairly impersonal gifts: place mats, a blanket, chocolate, picnic sets, jigsaws (the Queen's a big fan, and over the holidays there's always an infernally difficult jigsaw puzzle in progress on a table somewhere). Prankish gifts go down well in a family fond of practical jokes; one year Prince Andrew is said to have given everyone a Whoopee cushion. Charles goes for home-spun presents: preserves made from Highgrove fruit, or samples of essential oils that have been distilled from the rose and datura in his precious garden.

Supper's a light snack, perhaps smoked salmon and scrambled eggs, and some family members may settle down in another room with the latest video. (The palace requests them—and of course gets them—from major film companies soon after release, since the only time the royals ever get to go to the movies is for royal pre-mieres.) The Queen's been known to doze off if the plot isn't absolutely riveting, and Princess Alexandra gets em-barrassed and often sneaks out during sex scenes. For once, the children are always keen to get to bed, anx-iously awaiting a visit from Santa.

In the royal household, though, the true purpose of Christmas is never forgotten for long. There is a strong religious tradition—the Queen is head of the Church of England—and at midnight, anyone still awake joins the Queen for a Christmas carol service in the nearby church. Everyone also has to dress up in his or her best Christmas finery for another trip to church the following morning; there's simply no choice in the matter.

As in so many homes, the festivities kick off at the crack of dawn, with excited youngsters bouncing on their parents' bed and unpacking a present-filled stock-ing. William and Harry traditionally get a tangerine, chocolate money, and a host of inexpensive gifts that Diana has picked out herself at the toy store Hamley's; she's been spotted queuing to pay for toy gliders, footballs, and Teenage Mutant Ninja Turtles. (It seems even royal households aren't immune to those.) Prince Charles loves helping Diana put together stockings, and he does one for his wife and parents, too; in fact, all the adults get a few extra presents of fripperies like soap, candles, the latest best-seller, a Hermès scarf, or a cashmere muffler.

In the kitchens, the servants are already hard at work, cooking turkeys not only for the royals, but for the entire staff. The staff have their Christmas lunch in two sittings, eleven thirty A.M. and (for senior staff) at midday, while the family lounge around in the living room, playing cards or backgammon or putting new batteries in children's toys. Scarlet-liveried waiters and elegantly dressed serving maids bustle around, making sure that every royal plate is piled high while the food's still piping hot. The head chef has the honor of carving the family turkey, of which the Queen Mum, as the oldest guest, gets first helping. The turkey's accompanied by brussels sprouts, cranberry sauce, bread stuffing, roast potatoes, and little sausages wrapped in bacon. All present pull Christmas crackers, read out the awful mottoes, and put silly paper hats on their heads. Only the Queen refrains from this indignity; nothing less than a tiara or the Crown Jewels is ever allowed to muss *her* hairdo.

Lunch must be cleared away by three P.M for an important feature of the day: the Queen's televised speech. As in homes the length and breadth of the nation, this family watches intently while a habitually serious-looking Queen (wearing a gargantuan diamond brooch or two) recaps what the year has meant to her and what she feels the nation has achieved—and, if viewers are lucky, gives a glimpse behind the scenes. Past speeches have included fascinating insights into royal life, such as shots of Prince William chasing his cousin Zara around the room during Prince Harry's christening party, or film of the children petting the notoriously vicious royal corgis. Generally, though, the mood is serious. The Queen and Prince Philip then sneak off to watch the speech on their own, leaving everyone else to pass judgment; the couple return to the family fold when the broadcast's over to hear the (somewhat uncritical) verdict.

By then, though, everyone's complaining that they've eaten too much, which is hardly surprising: The royal Christmas is one long feast. (Diana feels the need to escape to the nearby health club whenever she can, to work off some of the excess calories notched up during the holidays.) The day has already started with a lavish breakfast—eggs, oatmeal, kippers (smoked fish), kedgeree (a fish-rice-and-egg dish), toast, and Fortnum & Mason marmalade—and there's tea still to come. So everyone bundles up against the cold and goes for a long, brisk walk. The rest of the day is theirs to fill as they please. The Queen and Prince Philip hand out gifts to their staff, to the value of about $35 a head, although there's an extra reward for long, loyal service.

The fourth meal of the day—supper—is served at about eight thirty: cold turkey and stuffing, salads, and potatoes. (With all this emphasis on food, it's no wonder that health freak Diana feels the urge to work on her figure extra hard after the annual Sandringham blowout. One January, while the royals were still languishing at Sandringham, she took herself off to spend a week with the mud packs and masseurs at Britain's most exclusive health spa, $4,000-a-week Champneys. Diana not only swam daily but sampled a wide range of exercise classes and beauty treatments—and restricted herself to the five-hundred-calorie-a-day "light diet" to restore her svelte figure after the excesses of the festive season.)

At Sandringham mealtimes, name cards indicate where everyone should sit; it's musical chairs, with new neighbors each meal. (Occasionally, if he's feeling mischievous, Prince Phillip will rearrange them and put Princess Michael and the Duchess of Kent together. Their mild bickering always amuses the rest of the family.) Then, after the children have been put to bed, some of the younger royals—including Diana, Fergie, Viscount Linley (Princess Margaret's son), and the viscount's sister, Lady Sarah Armstrong-Jones—like to join in the staff disco, rolling back the priceless carpet, getting down and getting funky with the footmen and chambermaids.

There's no sleeping-in the next day, though; breakfast, as usual, is served at eight thirty *sharp*. Friends are then invited to join the royals for a day of shooting on the Sandringham estate, with Prince Philip as host. (If it's your first visit, a member of the Queen's household will phone about a week before your arrival to establish your shoe size. In your room, you'll then find a pair of perfectly fitting green Hunter Wellington boots.)

Now that William is old enough to join in, Diana spends a few hours in her Wellies with the shooting party, enjoying a lavish picnic lunch, and then returns to her room, a good book, and some rare peace: For once, someone else is keeping both her sons entertained. By the end of the Christmas break Diana will be itching to get back to London. Tempers fray even in this family after a mere week or two cloistered together—and the Sandringham break can stretch on for six monotonous weeks, a haze of gunfire punctuated by picnic lunches, afternoon teas, and formal dinners. So relations between

Diana and the Queen have been known to get a little fractious.

While a great respecter of tradition, with a love of history, Diana is occasionally frustrated by the royals' stuffiness, their refusal, as she sees it, to get modern. Royal protocol is supposed to be followed at all times, and Diana has occasionally been frowned on by the Queen for cutting corners and breaking rules. (That old rebellious streak again?) The Queen is not used to having her authority challenged, but Diana is an efficent, modern woman who sometimes perceives that there's a better way of doing things. She has on more than one occasion suggested that something in the royal household be done in a new way, only to be met with a brusque "But, Your Highness, it's *always* been done this way." End of subject. Diana does behave more regally than many of the wilder, younger royals do, but, in her mother-in-law's house, at least, she can't be as informal as she might like.

Balmoral Castle is large enough for Diana to lose herself in, to stay out of the general fray, and occasionally, she is allowed to invite her family; her sister Jane is a frequent guest at Balmoral, because of her husband's job. But even that isn't enough to endow the place with much charm in Diana's eyes. It may well be that, having to take a place well down in the pecking order, after the Queen Mother, Princess Margaret, Prince Philip, and so on, Diana simply misses being mistress of her own home. In any case, this frustration makes it frankly impossible for Diana to endure the entire summer break at Balmoral. Four years in a row she has found more and more excuses to escape to London, piling her diary with work commitments—the only excuses the Queen accepts as legitimate for escape from the remote Scottish Highlands house that was once Queen Victoria's favorite and where things have pretty much been stuck in a time warp ever since. The late Lord Carlingford once likened staying at Balmoral to being in prison, and that's rather how Diana feels. There is windburn. There are mosquitoes. And there is boredom. Despite rumors of a royal rift, it isn't really that Diana doesn't want to spend time with Prince Charles—it's "that place." As a friend of Diana's explains, "for a country-bred girl, the princess is basically a townie at heart." When the going at Balmoral gets tough, Diana can't even go shopping: The local town offers little to fritter away her fortune on other than sensible leather sandals, thermal underwear, and kilts. Small wonder that in 1991, the Duchess of York declared that she was following Diana's lead and bowing out of all but a few days of the summer sojourn.

For Diana, the monotony at Balmoral isn't even broken by the arrival of an endless stream of guests. Outsiders are regularly asked to join the royal house party—a royal summons arrives via a stampless envelope or a telephone call from Lieutenant Colonel Blair Stewart-Wilson, deputy master of the household. Guests, who will be invited either because they work in a sphere that fascinates the royals or because someone has decided their job is funny, range from Mrs. Thatcher to Elton John. (Elton, strangely enough, is a regular royal intimate, a great favorite of the Queen Mother, and often turns up at royal gatherings. Once, on finding himself seated next to the Queen at dinner, the camp rock star leaned over to the person sitting next to him and whispered, "Not bad for a boy from Pinner!" But Elton's experiences just go to show what a minefield of manners being a royal guest can be. He once bowed to a lady who was not royal, and was so embarrassed that he couldn't meet her eye for the rest of the day.)

Why does the Queen love Balmoral so? Its remoteness, certainly. A fairly modern castle (it was completed in 1855), it is grand, resplendent with Landseer paintings, stuffed stags' heads, tartan wallpaper, tartan carpets— even tartan linoleum. There are 11,750 acres, with grouse moors for shooting; salmon fishing on the river Dee; golf; riding; and cricket. None of these is exactly up Diana's street. The food is apparently of ultra-gourmet standard: roast chicken, homegrown vegetables, sea bass, delicious sorbets and ices. There's nothing spicy, and absolutely *no* garlic; the royals are terrified of halitosis. Balmoral's downside is that few of the bedrooms have private baths, so the tenant has to take a long walk in a dressing gown down a drafty corridor. And there's no swimming pool, so Diana has to pack her towel and decamp to a local country hotel, usually overrun with tabloid journalists at this time of year.

Reveille is at eight thirty A.M., to the less-than-gentle strains of a bagpiper in a kilt, blowing his little heart out beneath the bedroom windows. Diana gets a merciful lie-in while the gents—in their tweedy plus fours—head for the grouse moors. She has the morning to putter, finishing paperwork or telephoning friends in London (although the Queen keeps an eagle eye on the itemized phone bill), before joining the party's stragglers in the castle's stone-flagged hall. The entourage, and the panting dogs, bundle into a Range Rover or two and head off to join the guns for a picnic served by the Queen herself on tartan blankets: "by Royal Appointment" sausages (kept piping hot in a special catering vehicle), flasks of tea and whiskey; sandwiches; and fruit. But despite the swarm of serving hands, guests are expected to join in the washing-up!

There are endless barbecues, too. As former royal chef Kevin Mitchell recalls, "Prince Philip takes on the role of chef and really enjoys himself. But they don't just take a few sandwiches in Tupperware boxes and chicken drumsticks. The prince has a Land Rover specially kitted out, with racks for the spices, hampers, steaks, and vintage wine. He personally always makes sure everything is loaded up properly, and often pops into the kitchens for his provisions."

The royals are accomplished hosts, and many testify to the feeling that they really care for their guests. If you're looking lonely or shy, a member of the family or a Lady of the Bedchamber—*someone,* anyhow—will appear out of the ether to put you at your ease. They like friends to leave having had a wonderful time—but they like, in exchange, to be amused themselves.

The great quandary shared by guests—one that fortunately doesn't trouble family member Diana—is what to give their hostess. Expense, of course, is not going to impress a person worth, at a rough estimate, $12 billion. "The secret is not to take chocolates," insists a veteran. "All the 'Sloane Rangers' take chocolates, because they are safe. But they'd prefer something from the outside world that they don't know about—like one of those Japanese dancing flowers, something like that!"

Diana's feelings toward Charles's family are mixed. She is always respectful to the Queen, and the two do get on well; Diana occasionally joins her mother-in-law for a light lunch or tea at Buckingham Palace. (But there's no dropping by; nobody, not even Charles, gets to see the Queen without an appointment.) Diana does, however, enjoy an easy and relaxed friendship with Princess Margaret, her fun-loving neighbor at Kensington Palace; Diana brings her bunches of flowers and baskets of homegrown raspberries from Highgrove, and the Waleses often dine with Margaret at K.P., which houses so many royal relations it's actually referred to as the aunt heap. Margaret has seen in Diana a kindred spirit, a woman who also finds the remorseless hunting-and-shooting life-style a crashing bore. Diana's become close, too, to Princess Margaret's children, carpenter extraordinaire Viscount Linley (who she invited along on her sons' first skiing holiday), and Lady Sarah Armstrong-Jones, who has always played down her royal position.

Diana enjoys an easy, teasing relationship with both of Charles's brothers: Andrew (who is eternally grateful for introducing him to his paramour, Sarah Ferguson), and theatrically minded Edward. Things are a little trickier with Princess Anne, who is famous for her brusqueness. Rumors of frostiness between the two arose when, on Harry's birth, Diana and Charles passed over Princess Anne in the choice of godparents. To deflect any talk of an estrangement, Diana felt compelled to explain in a television interview with Sir Alastair Burnet that "Princess Anne has been working incredibly hard for the Save the Children Fund, and I am her biggest fan, because what she crams into a day I could never achieve. We've hit it off very well and I just think she's marvelous." That may have been a slight exaggeration, but the two *have* mellowed toward each other, and Anne is grateful to Diana for stepping into the breach during her frequent overseas tours of duty, acting almost as surrogate mom to her kids, Peter and Zara Phillips, who in turn dote on Diana. They've had a tough time lately; their father, Mark Phillips (who'd recently separated from his royal wife) was the subject of a bolt-from-the-blue paternity suit from a blond New Zealand equestrian; Diana made sure that, as usual, she was on hand to take the children's minds off their family breakdown and the ensuing press frenzy.

The event in the annual royal calendar that Diana *does* love is Ascot, in June. It gives her the perfect excuse to commission a week's worth of beautiful new clothes from Catherine Walker, since the fashion watchers are out in droves and Diana must live up to their expectations. Windsor Castle, where the week's festivities take place, is close enough to throbbing London for Diana to feel close to the action—and besides, Ascot offers her the opportunity to see *all* her aristocratic friends, who apply in February for their exclusive passes to the royal enclosure, where movie stars rub shoulders with millionaires and royals.

The Queen and the Queen Mother are passionate racegoers and have owned hundreds of winners between them. Diana's more interested in the social and sartorial side of things. But during Ascot Week, the Queen seems to like to surround herself with a younger crowd, and the minor royals are allowed to invite friends to stay, or simply to lunch in the royal box. It was to cheer up Fergie (then suffering the agony of a crumbling, dead-end relationship with older man Paddy McNally) that Cupid Diana invited her flame-haired friend to the Ascot Week house party and kindled another royal romance. At lunch, Prince Andrew realized that he'd met his match in the fun department. As a then-overweight Sarah recalled, "He made me eat chocolate profiteroles, which I didn't want to eat at all. I was meant to be on a diet!" "So I got hit!" Andrew insisted later. During the years when their friendship was still close, Diana certainly relished having Fergie's company at Ascot; nowadays, since

Sarah is automatically invited (and relations between the princess and the duchess, while not icy, have definitely cooled), Diana's more likely to invite her friend Catherine Soames, who was married to Charles's friend Nicholas Soames.

In the year's calendar, there are other dates (like the Trooping of the Colour, the State Opening of Parliament, and the Remembrance Day parade) that Diana must mark in her diary. She must also turn up, sparkling and dripping with diamonds, for visits by overseas dignitaries and foreign royals. Certain invitations are marked "MOTG"—royal shorthand for "morally obliged to go," meaning Diana's presence is not just expected, it's demanded. At Buckingham Palace alone, the Queen hosts over eighty functions a year, from small, informal lunches, to the three garden parties with their nine-thousand-person guest lists. All in all, the Queen entertains over 40,000 people during the space of a year—and they're all just itching for a glimpse of Diana.

Banquets at Buckingham Palace, however, are truly regal affairs; the starched damask table linen is almost blindingly white. Guests eat from monogrammed china, using gold knives and forks (and are often plunged into panic over whether they're using the correct ones). The flowers are staggering; "horticultural artist" Kenneth Turner, famous for his over-the-top floral decorations (often incorporating fruit and vegetables in the arrangements, for a dash of originality) is a favorite with all the royal hostesses, and the bill for petals alone may run into the thousands.

The drinks are usually chosen by wine buff Prince Philip from the well-stocked vintage cellar (and will usually start with Mumm de Mumm champagne), but the food is notoriously simple fare, designed to appeal to the average palate—simple roasts and grills, fresh vegetables—and *no* oysters, milk puddings, or, of course, garlic. Ices made from pulped fresh fruit are a favorite dessert, followed by handmade chocolates, which delight chocoholic Diana. At her own table, she's been known to polish off almost a yard of Bendick's rich bittermints single-handed!

These official dinners and cocktail parties are when Diana truly gets to dazzle. Out come the tiara and the extravagant jewels, one aspect of Diana's life-style that has most of us turning green with envy. Although in her daily life Diana prefers a low-key look, wearing a small pair of gold earrings and her diamond-and-sapphire engagement ring (she hates being ostentatious about wealth when moving among the underprivileged), she truly gets to sparkle at official dinners, wearing jewels that reflect her own taste and style. Unlike older royal ladies, who sometimes drip with diamond-laden diadems, tiaras, necklaces, and brooches—and end up looking like Christmas trees—Diana has a bolder, simpler, and, as a result, far more dramatic style. She feels that the Queen's baubles, bangles, and bijoux are a trifle middle-aged, even though one day we shall see *Diana* shine in Crown Jewels such as the Diamond Diadem, Queen Victoria's emerald bracelet, and the celebrated Victorian bow brooches.

Since she first met Charles, Diana has been showered in glorious jewels, from her £28,500 engagement ring on. It's a priceless perk of the job. Appropriately enough, one of Johnny Spencer's wedding presents to his daughter was an empty jewel box—not that Diana was a stranger to glittering baubles: For her wedding, she wore the beautiful Spencer tiara. But her wedding present from the Queen was a magnificent diamond tiara of her own, which once belonged to the Queen's grandmother Queen Mary. It is a tall crescent of diamond-encrusted lover's knots, from which hang nineteen perfect pearl tears. But it's hellishly heavy, and Diana's lady-in-waiting knows to carry aspirin or a homeopathic equivalent, in case carrying that terrific weight on her head during an entire evening of small talk with awestruck diplomats or dignitaries gives Di a crushing headache.

Not everything the princess is given is quite to her taste. And rather than smile politely, grit her teeth, and wear a jewel she considers vulgar or outmoded, Diana has the perfect answer: She has it reset. The Queen Mother's lavish gift to her new granddaughter-in-law, for instance, was a giant sapphire brooch surrounded by diamonds—just the sort of priceless trinket of which the royals are traditionally so fond. Diana wore it just once, to a state banquet, and then had her jewelers rework it, mounting it in seven strings of perfect pearls so that she could wear it as a choker around her swanlike neck.

Another wedding gift was similarly dismantled. When Crown Prince Abdullah of Saudi Arabia gave Diana a breathtaking sapphire necklace-bracelet-and-earring set as a wedding gift, Diana was so shocked she gasped, "Gosh, I don't even know the man!" The pendant necklace stayed, as did the bracelet and earrings, but the ring was so like her own engagement ring that she swapped it for a watch face (she was given three watches at the time of her wedding), to make an original bracelet.

That was Diana's first taste of the generosity of foreign royals—particularly Middle Easterners—although she has never quite been able to get over being presented gems worth literally millions, a not-so-discreet thank-you for visiting someone's country. A diamond-encrusted gold choker and earrings from Saudi Arabia's King Fahd, for instance, are said to be worth a million pounds. Another Middle Eastern potentate bestowed on her a cascade of diamonds and rubies with matching earrings. (During the Gulf conflict, however, to prevent any embarrassment, these gifts from oil-rich nations stayed firmly under lock and key.)

Foreign bigwigs have, in fact, fallen over themselves to outdo each other in the royal gift stakes ever since the days of the empire, when the royal family was proffered an embarrassment of riches—diamonds, rubies, emeralds, and pearls—from eager Indian royal houses. Diana is simply the latest in a long line of lucky recipients. But although these gifts are rarely seen on Diana, they can't be broken up for fear of offending. Instead, they must be noted down and stored away, brought out if the dignitary pays a visit to the U.K. or Charles and Di make a return trip to visit their oh-so-generous hosts.

Naturally, the younger royals are keeping up the tradition of commissioning jewels. Their patronage, down the years, has ensured that many British (and French) jewelery businesses have thrived. For Di's twenty-first birthday, Charles went to designer Leo de Vroomen to find something dramatic for his wife; he settled on a necklace of black and white pearls, interspersed with black enamel cubes that were each set with a black baroque pearl. But it was too avant-garde for the princess; she had a quiet word with Charles, and he let her remove the cubes. Since then, she's worn it often. There have been other occasions when Diana has, famously, shown her originality with jewels. Suffering form sunburn in Australia, she couldn't face the agony of wearing her emerald-and-diamond necklace, so she wore it as a headband instead, a stylish trick that earned her front-page space in newspapers around the world.

For official occasions Diana can dip into the royal vaults and (after the Queen and Queen Mother have had their pick) take what she fancies—although these aren't the Crown Jewels, which are locked up in the Tower of London and only brought out for state occasions. Top London jewelers, only too glad to have their creations displayed on a royal model, have been known to lend important pieces, too. But in fact, no matter what the occasion, you'd never catch Diana flaunting her jewels to a group of people as Fergie did after her engagement, gasping "Clock the rocks!"

It's never easy, acquiring a set of in-laws—but few of us have to learn *quite* as much as Diana did in order to be accepted by our husband's family. Being royal in the nineties means showing dignity and decorum, abiding by the royal rules and regulations (at least most of the time)—and putting your own desires second. Until the day, that is, when the royal roost is ruled by Queen Diana. And *then*, perhaps, they'll be changing traditions at Buckingham Palace.

# 4

# From Frump to Fabulous

*P*recious few British women are deemed chic enough to earn a coveted place on Eleanor Lambert's famous "best-dressed list." Fewer still make it into the "Best-Dressed Hall of Fame," immortalized forever as icons of chic. But almost every year for the past few years, one name has cropped up at the top of the list: that of the Princess of Wales, who, Cinderella-style, has been transformed from a down-home nursery-school teacher into a paragon of soignée elegance. Indeed, when 1991's list appeared, with Diana's name scratched from it, insiders insisted that it was merely "to give someone else a break for a change."

Of course, I hear you say, with the princess's dress allowance—around $200,000 annually—it would be a breeze to ensure you ranked up there with Paloma Picasso, Nancy Reagan, and Jackie Kennedy Onassis. But even having all that cash to splash out on new designer clothes won't necessarily clinch it for you, as many an overdressed Texan "trophy wife" knows to her chagrin. You must also have that elusive quality: real style. And nowadays, that's something POW (as friends call her) projects every time she steps into the limelight.

It wasn't always that way, of course. Eleanor Lambert, originator of the celebrated list, would barely have given a glance to Diana in her shy Sloane Ranger days or the early moments of her courtship (when she was once seen scurrying to Princess Margaret's fiftieth birthday party with a heavy green loden overcoat casually flung over her flouncy, glittering evening dress). Diana's family's dressmaker, Bill Pashley, a favorite of her mother and sisters, maintains that "she was always interested in clothes and had a strong eye for color and a sense of style."

That didn't keep Diana from making plenty of mistakes, however—all of them, to her embarrassment, in public; next morning, over her cornflakes, the evidence would be glaring at her from the front page of every paper (at that time hungry for any crumb of news about the Prince of Wales's future bride). How she must have blushed upon seeing shots of herself emerging from a limousine at London's Goldsmiths Hall for her very first official evening engagement, one dainty pink nipple peeking from the overly low-cut bodice of her black taffeta ball gown. What's more, it was evident that nobody at the palace had briefed Diana about a crucial point of royal etiquette: Royals don't wear black, except during periods of mourning (a rule that was to be the source of some frustration for Diana, since during much of the next five years most chic women wore nothing but).

Someone should have told her, too, that the matronly, cornflower-blue five-hundred-dollar suit that she chose off the rack (from Harrods) for her engagement photos would have looked better on a woman twice—perhaps even three times—her age. Certainly, looking at those photographs of the blushing ingenue (anxious, as she flaunted her engagement ring, that the world might notice that she bit her nails), it is hard to believe she's the same Diana who today exudes confidence and chic from every perfectly made-up pore.

Early on in her marriage, too, Diana seemed to be having trouble finding her fashion feet (although, with two pregnancies, even *seeing* her feet was a bit of a problem a good part of the time). Pie-crust frill collars, sailor suits, and billowing silk skirts were hardly destined to catapult her to the ranks of world-class style setters. As time has worn on, however, Diana has discovered her own signature style—with a little help from her friends: her dressers, the designers themselves, and two fashion experts, *Vogue*'s Felicity Clark and Anna Harvey, enlisted to do a makeover on nineteen-year-old Diana Spencer in time for her wedding. Their first meeting marked a turning point for Diana and set her on the path to total transformation.

Diana's elder sister Lady Jane Fellowes once worked at British *Vogue* magazine: Lady Jane recalled her former colleagues' reputation for having their fingers firmly on the fashion pulse and made a gentle inquiry as to whether Miss Clark and Miss Harvey might be prepared to give Diana a little "guidance." Soon afterward, Diana made her first visit to *Vogue*'s Hanover Square H.Q., in the center of London's West End shopping district. The chic trio continued to meet there for girlish chat and dressing-up sessions until the prince's security-conscious advisers suggested that, in order to avoid potential terrorist threats, the talks should be shifted to Buckingham

Palace (and later, after the wedding itself, to Diana's new home at Kensington Palace).

As a result of these style consultations, Diana was introduced to Britain's design elite: Jan Vanvelden, David Sassoon of Bellville Sassoon, Jasper Conran, Arabella Pollen, Caroline Charles, Bruce Oldfield, Jacques Azagury, and Victor Edelstein, all of whom leaped at the opportunity to dress a woman regarded as the ultimate, publicity-generating clotheshorse. Indeed, until relatively recently, Anna Harvey would still point the princess in the direction of designers she thought Diana would like, sometimes cabbing clothes or accessories—wrapped in oceans of rustling tissue paper—to Kensington Palace for approval.

But as time wore on, Diana began to grow more self-assured and daring, setting styles as well as following them. There was the time she borrowed her husband's tuxedo for a Prince's Trust pop concert, and another occasion when she teamed his bow tie with a striking, brass-buttoned Royal Hampshire Regiment officer's jacket. POW-er dressing was born. Diana reveled in her high-profile "Di-nasty" phase, flirting with designers' creations and grabbing global headlines with Joan Collins–style shoulder pads and razzle-dazzle off-the-shoulder sequins.

Stories of her spending—and her husband's disapproval—became legend. According to rumors, Diana was racking up as much as $400,000 in annual dress bills—and that was *after* the hefty discount her designers are only too delighted to offer. It's fine to marry one of the world's wealthiest men—but not to be perceived to be squandering his stash. The British public, conscious that they pay Prince Charles's hefty salary every year, began to whisper of reckless extravagance.

Diana reportedly arrived on the tarmac in Australia, for instance, for one official tour, accompanied by no less than ninety trunks, featuring the creations of twenty-one designers. "Well," she rationalized later, "it was when we first went on tour after we got married. I had to buy endless new things, of course, because on a tour you change three or four times a day. That was the problem," she continued. "The arrival of all the new things was causing tremendous criticism, but what else could I do? I couldn't go around in a leopard skin!"

Later on, it was reported that for a trip to Italy Diana had lavished $150,000 on new outfits. But in Milan, the princess had the last laugh, turning up for a gala performance at the La Scala opera house in a favorite Victor Edelstein pink gown, worn several times before—definitely an "I'll show 'em" gesture, targeted at her critics. The Italian press was furious that Diana hadn't worn the anticipated avalanche of stunning new outfits (which were later brought out, one by one, back home). When taken to task on the subject, Diana declared: "Well, I'm afraid you're going to see everything time and time again, because it fits, it's comfortable, and it works. You know, I think a lot of people thought that I was going on a fashion tour for two weeks, but I wasn't. I was going along to support the British flag, with my husband, as his wife. My clothes were far from my mind."

Around that time, Diana began to feel that she couldn't win. She opened her heart to friends on the subject. The criticism targeted at her had most definitely stung. "If I dress the part, I'm accused of extravagance," she lamented to a member of her circle. "If I wear something several times, people say, 'That old thing again.' " It wasn't long before Diana reached a sensible equilibrium, though; much-loved outfits that make her feel like a million are worn repeatedly, as she predicted. Some cast-off outfits that *aren't* so successful are passed on to her similarly sized sisters or to friends. For a while, some cast-offs found their way into Fergie's wardrobe, before *her* marriage. Diana has also become a mistress of the art of "make do and mend," with the nimble-fingered assistance of her seamstresses, who constantly rework outfits by changing sleeve designs or buttons, or alter the length of many outfits so that the public, and the princess herself, don't get bored with them. It's a clever way to deflect the flak intermittently aimed at her.

Anyone who points a finger accusingly at Diana's spending, however, might like to reflect on the boost she's given the British fashion industry, which, until she arrived on the scene, had been in the doldrums since the late sixties. Both upmarket and mass-market fashion businesses have flourished. Copycat clothing companies have made a fat buck riding on the backs of her designers. For a while, whenever Diana appeared in public, her outfits would be sketched by rapid-fire copyists; the results would appear in Britain's stores within days, where Diana wannabes would snap them up delightedly.

Perhaps unsurprisingly, not long after the Italian episode Diana started to complain that whenever she appeared in public, people were more interested in what she was wearing than what she was doing—more than a little galling, no doubt, when you're devoting most of your waking hours to raising money for charity, or bringing a little cheer into the lives of old people or AIDS patients. She vowed that a new, simpler look was called for—still reeling, no doubt, from criticism of one particular Rifat Ozbek "circus" outfit, about which critics sniffed: "She looked more like a pantomime principal boy than Britain's Queen of Style." More and more,

Diana began to turn to French-born designer Catherine Walker of the Chelsea Design Company, whose creations are among the most elegant available in the United Kingdom, for her day and evening wear.

Gossip has it, in fact, that a highly successful TV program—"The Clothes Show," watched by millions and rumored to be a must-see program at Kensington Palace—may have had a part to play in Diana's metamorphosis. Diana noted the name of talented milliner Philip Somerville after watching an item about him on "The Clothes Show." She's always had a problem finding hats to suit, and decided that Somerville's designs were just what she needed to complete the new, ultra-simple look created in tandem with Catherine Walker.

So, with the serendipitous discovery of Catherine Walker and Philip Somerville, Diana embraced a new look—one that I predict she'll stick to forever, because (just as she'd hoped) it enables her personality to shine through; and that, surely, is something anyone who's had the sneaking feeling that her dress was wearing *her* can identify with. Interestingly, what has virtually become Diana's uniform owes little to fashion; for proof, look at Diana's knee- or ankle-grazing hemlines, at a time when skirt lengths in general (and her sister-in-law's, in particular) are soaring skyward. (But then, as Diana herself has reportedly said, "You can't have hems too short because when you bend over there are six children looking up your skirt.") The image Diana has now embraced transcends the shifting sands of style, catapulting her into the realms of the truly chic.

Like many Frenchwomen, Catherine Walker seems to have been born with chic. But there are other qualities that enable this beautiful brunette to design seemingly intuitively for Diana: Both women are tall, slim, and shy.

Notoriously low-profile and discreet, fortyish Catherine never set her heart on a design career; dressmaking was merely a passionate hobby until her (English) husband died, at the tragically young age of thirty-two, of a heart attack. It was partly to assuage her grief and partly to earn a living that Catherine Walker threw herself full-time into designing; in fact, she admits, "it saved my sanity in the months after John's death." But her "Chelsea set" friends soon discovered the allure of Catherine's understated designs, and in 1977 a new design star was born.

When Diana met up with her, ten years after that debut, Catherine was the answer to a fashion prayer, offering the princess styles created with all the savoir faire of a French couturier but essentially homegrown. Although privately indulging a love for foreign designers, particularly Mondi, Escada, and Ralph Lauren— ordered over the telephone from catalogues—Diana considers it her patriotic duty to back her country's fashion industry by appearing only in British designs while on duty. But Diana does insist that boosting English designers' fortunes isn't her prime consideration. She's said, "Obviously, if I'm helping the fashion industry and helping the British side of things, well, that's marvelous—but I never tried to do that. And," adds the princess, always eager to carve out a more serious image for herself these days, "I do think there's too much emphasis altogether on my clothes."

Secretly, Diana would love to flaunt the designs of foreign designers. She apparently grew quite envious when Sarah jetted off to Paris after her marriage to the Duke of York to fill her wardrobe with the creations of Yves Saint Laurent and Chanel. But it would definitely be considered bad form if Diana were to follow her sister-in-law's lead in public. She has only felt free to wear Continental designers when she's traveling to their home countries. For a trip to Germany, she wore a bold yellow-and-black-checked coat by Escada, and on a trip to France in 1988, for one glorious day, she was able to flaunt top-to-toe Chanel, in homage to that country's legendary couturière.

Bernadette Rendall, the elegant Frenchwoman who runs Chanel in London, recalls the time when she was summoned to Kensington Palace to help plan Diana's outfit. Rendall took with her a video of the latest show; very rich, very select Chanel clients watch the exclusive video, which comes in its stylish black box, in the comfort of their own boudoirs. "The princess knew exactly which item she wanted, and how she wanted to wear it," recalls Madame Rendall of the bright red wool bouclé coat that stole the show in France.

In the video, Karl Lagerfeld's then-favorite model Inès de la Fressange wore the coat over gray pants, a blouse, and a necktie, but Diana preferred a simpler neckline and insisted on a skirt; pants are a definite no-go for Diana's daywear. "I suggested a few pieces, but the final choice was hers—the gray flannel skirt and a round-necked satin blouse with a single-button trim." Chanel seamstresses had two fittings to shorten the ensemble to Diana's preferred length. Then Rendall suggested Diana complete her outfit with the classic chain-handle quilted bag. She leaped at the opportunity to acquire this status symbol, coveted by women all over the world. "Well, I don't really need somewhere to keep my keys and passport," smiled the princess, "but why not!" With a pair of distinctive pearl-and-gilt earrings and a pair of leather pumps, the princess seemed to revel in "my indulgence in Chanel," as she described it.

But the ensemble was a great choice; when she wore it in France, she stole the show and won the hearts of the French people.

Diana has only once been seen in Chanel since: Unexpectedly, she wore a navy Chanel suit for an official engagement in England, to lay a foundation stone at Great Ormond Street Hospital, whose fund-raising she'd headed. Observes an insider, "She just felt like a rebel that morning, and thought, 'To hell with protocol, for once!' " Alternatively, she may simply have been testing the waters, to find out whether the British public really minded if she flew the tricolor, rather than the Union Jack, for a change. She got her answer; in the next morning's newspaper, a spokeswoman for British designer Helen Storey wailed, "It's a tragedy!"

A great passion of Diana's is dressing like a man. For years, she would borrow Prince Charles's $110 Trumbull & Asser shirts, until he put his foot down. And now, when she wants to turn heads and grab headlines, she still knows exactly how to do it: cross-dressing—in the best possible taste. Visiting members of the armed forces is an important element of Diana's work, and she likes almost nothing better than to become one of the boys for the day. She had donned a jaunty naval cap to visit sailors at the Dartmouth naval base, and when a visit to the Royal Hampshire Regiment (where she holds the rank of colonel-in-chief) was scheduled, she had one of their combat uniforms specially tailored. Close inspection of her flak jacket revealed that shoulder pads had been added, while her trousers were taken in, the better to flaunt her long, slender legs. She became an instant pinup for the troops, flattered by her stylish gesture.

But it is really Diana's Catherine Walker–designed day wardrobe, recognizable at a hundred paces for its clean lines and fabulous fabrics (principally wool and silk), the only detailing large buttons in brass and mother-of-pearl, that has scooped international fashion awards. Whenever a foreign tour is scheduled, it is to Walker that Diana turns—and her favorite couturière invariably comes up trumps with outfits to wow 'em in the Arab states, Italy, or America. Mrs. Walker's designs *are* expensive—about $1,200 for a day dress, $2,500 for a suit, and up to $6,000 for a made-to-measure evening gown (and Di's got plenty of those, too)—but Diana has discovered, to her delight, that dressing with Mrs. Walker saves her time and money (and not just because of the generous discount she's reputed to get). About 80 percent of her clothes now come from this single source: countless smart suits (bellhop style is a popular favorite) and coat-dresses, as well as silk, satin, or brocade evening gowns by the dozen, now hang in her Kensington Palace walk-in closet (presided over by her two dressers, Fay Marshalsea and Evelyn Dagley).

The very simplicity of the Chelsea Design Company look enables Diana to wear her clothes time and again, without giving the impression that she's only got half a dozen outfits to her name. She never feels, "Oh, not *that* old thing again" with a Catherine Walker design. She's mastered "investment dressing," something many of us—prone to falling for fleeting fashions and wearing them twice before boredom sets in—could usefully learn. In fact, though some might think her spending on clothes to be recklessly extravagant, Diana has a strong thrifty streak: Catherine's designs are often reworked after they've been worn too often, reappearing in an even simpler guise. Milliner Philip Somerville frequently tinkers with her headgear, subtly altering its appearance, and confirms: "She thinks about each outfit, where she can wear it and how often. She knows that if you keep to a classic look you can wear the same hat with lots of things, so a designer creation isn't really expensive at all."

The time-saving element is equally vital, however. Diana has, quite simply, decided that there are better ways to spend her valuable hours than standing around being fitted for frocks; she devotes an increasing amount of time to her work, and anything left over she prefers to reserve for her family—in particular, the boisterous William and Harry. Gone are the days when, as one hatmaker, a former favorite of Diana's, recalls, "I had to take one particular hat for *four* fittings—which, frankly, was over the top; nobody needs four fittings for a hat! But the princess seemed to lap up the attention." Insiders report that Diana, although still deeply concerned about looking her best, asks for videos of her favored designers' collections and has the minimum number of fittings, now that her size 10 figure never fluctuates by more than a half-inch here or there. To save even more time, when Diana spots something she loves, she orders it—Jackie Onassis–style—in a rainbow of colors; she owns one particular classic coat-dress in seven different colors and fabrics.

Catherine Walker's intimate knowledge of Diana's shape and measurements saves endless fittings (which, for added convenience, are usually carried out at K.P.). Not that the princess's style comes only from Walker. With growing confidence, she expresses her own ideas. Says Walker, "The princess often comes in with definite suggestions about what she wants, and we just make them up."

But practicality, as much as style, is of paramount importance to the princess: beneath the sleek designs you might well find her muffled against biting winds in thermal underwear, and she sticks to flat or low-heeled shoes, from Rayne, Charles Jourdan, and Pied-à-Terre. Finding shoes that are easy on her size 9A feet is essential; Diana spends as much time standing up each day as the average department-store saleswoman. There are other considerations, too, that you and I are lucky enough not to have to fret about; as Diana herself observes: "I can't always wear what I'd like to an engagement, because it's just not practical. There is only one golden rule. Clothes are for the job. They've got to be practical." That rules out linen, for instance, which creases too badly; sarong-style skirts won't do, either, since a wayward gust of wind can whip them open to reveal the royal unmentionables.

These days, even when Diana does opt to wear clothes by other designers, she invariably falls for their simplest—but nevertheless stunning—styles. Bruce Oldfield, credited with putting the oomph into Diana's wardrobe in the mid-eighties by encouraging her to wear figure-skimming styles, hasn't been forgotten. A soft-spoken designer from humble beginnings (he was raised in an orphanage), he is known to have dined privately with the Waleses, and Diana has a soft spot for both him and his work.

Another hardy perennial is Victor Edelstein, probably the U.K.'s top evening-wear designer, who has abandoned ready-to-wear and now works only on made-to-measure couture gowns in his South Kensington mews atelier. Edelstein's gowns are truly fit for a princess: Hems are weighted, fabrics the best that money can buy. As New York socialite Cece Kieselstein-Cord explains, "I've never met anyone who has the ability to make a dress fit like Victor. He only fits you one time. I never even try it on before I'm going to wear it. He's become one of the most important European designers in America, in couture. I think he's much better than Lacroix."

Edelstein is notoriously tight-lipped on the subject of his most celebrated client (although he did once privately admit to me that he didn't know how the princess could stand living her life in such a fishbowl). He will say, however, that "when I design, I have a thirty-year-old woman in my mind, a married woman. I think allure is what one's after; but there's a big difference between sexiness and tartiness. The main consideration is that a dress must be flattering. You want to be able to put it on and there it is—without having to start yanking it."

Edelstein remains a favorite with the princess, probably because his style philosophy seems to dovetail so neatly with hers: "You mustn't make a person feel like a cabaret when they go out," he explains. "You must bring fantasy and invention to clothes, but not so that they're demanding to wear. When a woman puts a dress on, it's got to make her feel wonderful." So every dress is fitted to perfection, lined with silk and interlined with floaty organza, so that not one stitch of the hem shows. And of the princess herself, Edelstein says, "She likes body-conscious clothes, and why not? She's got the figure."

He's dead right there. Princess Michael of Kent once remarked—probably through gritted teeth—that the Princess of Wales "would look good in a sack." And of course, her pencil-slim figure—worked on religiously with a personal trainer and early-morning swims at Buckingham Palace—shows off everything to flattering perfection. (Surprisingly, though, Diana's measurements are 35-29-35, revealing a very boyish, rather than model-ish shape). Diana knows that she literally can't afford to pile on the pounds; not only would she be faced with the horrible reality of her excess avoirdupois glaring out from every press picture, but just imagine the cost of investing in a whole new closetful of clothes.

Some of Diana's favorite clothes are rumored to be the ones she wears off-duty, when the pressure to look good 100 percent of the time is blissfully relaxed. She is always relieved to have time off from being a fashion plate. Smart, classic separates from Ralph Lauren, Mondi, Escada, and Planet are slowly bringing the princess's private wardrobe up to the high level of chic we have come to expect from her. Mondi is a particular favorite—she wears an inky blue Mondi baseball jacket constantly—and she's encouraged friends to seek out the label, too, insisting that "they are really good value for money," just as if she were any ordinary young mom-of-two on a tight budget. She loves shorts, too, and thinks nothing of turning up for lunch at Le Caprice, a frequent royal haunt, in a khaki jacket and Girl Scout shorts.

The princess now has little spare time for shopping, but on occasion has been known to pop into boutiques—with her private detective in tow for a second opinion! Harvey Nichols is her favorite department store; she was once spotted emerging from the changing room in a clinging leopard-print design by Patrick Kelly. "Do you think it's too tight?" she giggled. The bodyguard nodded. "Good, then I'll buy it!" declared the princess, leaving him to pick up the tab for her sexy new dress with a Duchy of Cornwall American Express card.

She has a penchant for the ultra-casual—baseball caps, jeans, outsize football jackets (complete with team name emblazoned across the back), bobby socks (sometimes worn with heels)—all of which she frequently mixes and mismatches with classics. Sometimes the look works, sometimes it doesn't—but at least Di no longer makes glaring style errors, like the famous occasion on which she arrived to see *The Phantom of the Opera* (for the third time) in a hideously uncoordinated combination of black satin bomber jacket, demure ruffled blouse, and red leather trousers worn with high heels. The overall effect was a bizarre mixture of Margaret Thatcher and a roadie from a Bon Jovi tour, and it contrasted painfully with her previous evening's fashion triumph: breathtaking flamenco flounces teamed with one black satin glove, one red.

Perhaps, on the occasion of her visit to *Phantom*, she had given both of her dressers the evening off. Evelyn Dagley and Fay Marshalsea have the responsibility of caring for the princess's clothes. The trio put their heads together months in advance to plan what Diana will be wearing to work; only dramatic weather conditions alter their schedule. When Diana wakes in the morning, her clothes are all ready for her: shoes polished, any repairs complete, the clothes laid out with matching accessories. Everything must look immaculate, so royal evening dresses are dispatched to Tothills in South East London to be dry-cleaned (at about $140 a pop). Her ecology-conscious husband has decreed that all royal laundry must be done with an environmentally friendly detergent, which takes care of some cotton blouses and the underwear. (She has a penchant for gray silk by Janet Reger or La Perla, and rumor has it she's lavished over $27,000 on frillies since her wedding.)

Clothes are stored on padded hangers, protected from

the threat of munching moths by special, mono-grammed covers supplied by the Knightsbridge store Eximous, a favorite in Diana's circle for its selection of personalized gifts. When Diana wears an outfit on official duty, her dressers note every detail in a record book.

Incidentally, the three have a fairly relaxed relationship. Fay Marshalsea is particularly fond of her boss, who stood by her through a period of serious illness a few years back. Fay was just getting excited about her upcoming wedding to RAF officer Stephen Appleby, when medical tests on a troublesome lump under her tongue turned up a diagnosis of cancer. The princess's loyal dresser was naturally heartbroken, but bit back the tears to go through with the most important day of her life; Diana was the guest of honor, but kept a low profile so as not to upstage the bride.

Less than a month later, Fay became too ill to carry out her responsibilities at Kensington Palace. But Diana found time in her hectic schedule to accompany Fay to the hospital, and offered her a bed in her own Kensington Palace apartment because of its proximity to the outpatient unit where Fay's daily chemotherapy and radiation treatment took place. During the day, Diana would drop in for a cup of tea and a gossip, and naturally, held Fay's job open. "She knew of my illness right from the start," recalls Fay (who, doctors believe, has now made a full recovery). "She is very close to me and I wanted to tell her. She gave me encouragement to carry on. She is a lovely person to work for, and very special to me. She just wanted to be there to support me. When I was ill, she was always either seeing me or asking after me.

Even before she had Evelyn and Fay to ensure that she always looks immaculate, Diana was a stickler for grooming; as a bachelor girl, she once used to supplement her living by starching and ironing shirts for merchant banker William Van Straubenzee. Since she met Charles, however, she has learned that if you're a princess, appearances are vital. As she observes: "Imagine having to go to a wedding every day, as the bride. That's what it's like." Diana is H.R.H. Cover Girl, and even after a decade in the job, just putting her picture on the front of a magazine guarantees soaring sales. As seasoned photographer Anwar Hussein explains, "Photography has played a far greater part in reshaping Diana's image than the written word." And Diana has been a willing accomplice; she has ensured that at all times, she looks every inch the perfect princess. Robin Nunn, another Rat Pack photographer, declares, "There are no flies on Diana. I can't remember the time she was last caught off guard." Or looking anything but wonderful.

The Rat Pack, who have all fallen under her spell, agree that Diana has learned how to make their task easier—even if, at times, she has resented the fact that they dog her every step. She will pause for the necessary photo opportunities during the day. She will hold a smile if necessary. And she (almost) always looks like a fashion plate straight from her adored *Vogue* magazine, to which she owes such a debt.

Surely, nobody could deny that Diana has earned her place in the Best-Dressed Hall of Fame. But en route to elegance, the princess has learned some useful lessons, which we might all well heed if we wish to dress like a Princess—albeit on a more slender budget! Despite the occasional glaring mistake, she has divined what suits her: the simplest, most pared down of clothes, with no fancy details or fussiness. And now that her passion for high fashion has given way to a love of clean-lined, classic clothes, Diana ensures that what the public sees when they flock for a glimpse of the POW is the woman beneath the wardrobe. These days, Diana wants to be known as a workhorse, not a clotheshorse.

# 5

# *Fit for Anything*

*I*t isn't just genes that keep aristocratic Diana looking good—it's damned hard work. From the moment when word of her romance leaked out and Diana first saw the pictures of her plump self splashed across the newspapers, she vowed to look as good as she possibly could—for her prince, for her public, but most of all for herself. Diana was embarrassed by the chubby cheeks, somewhat matronly waistline, and mousy hair she saw. Others were enchanted by her innocence and girlish looks, but not Diana. She couldn't focus on her good points, such as her long, shapely legs, but could see only her flaws. Diana vowed to change. And *fast*.

While not exactly Jane Fonda, Diana had always been pretty fit. As a girl, she dreamed of becoming a ballerina—an ambition thwarted when she neared her height of 5'10". As she confessed to one of the prima ballerinas at the London City Ballet Company, "I actually wanted to be a dancer, but overshot the height by a long way."

(Diana's a patron of the company, acknowledged as one of her favorite causes; she has been known to drop in unannounced to watch rehearsals avidly, if a shade wistfully.) But the love of dancing has stayed with her, and she shows off her prowess on the dance floor at the slightest opportunity—during private parties at the London nightclub Annabel's, at the Casa in Klosters, or at friends' weddings.

When Diana first moved into Buckingham Palace while final touches were being put to her future home, she took up tap dancing, enjoying lessons in the palace's grand Throne Room, where the Queen bestows honors on members of the nation's elite. The wooden floor was perfect for Diana's practice sessions. Her two dancing teachers—Wendy Vickers and seventy-seven-year-old Lily Snipp—together developed a routine that worked for Diana. It combines jazz, Latin American, and tap, and she can throw herself into it even in her teachers' absence, with her precious Walkman pounding out anything from Michael Jackson to Dire Straits.

Prince Charles admires his wife's skills, but he isn't, alas, blessed with enough of a sense of rhythm to match her high standards. When, at official functions (particularly on tour), Charles and Diana are forced to open the evening's dancing, Charles secretly cringes with embarrassment as he and his wife go through their well-rehearsed "jive-rock" routine. His pet hate is having to twirl Diana around in front of a horde of cameramen. "I can assure you," he has said, "it makes the heart sink to have to make an awful exhibition of ourselves."

On occasion, Charles has been known to take the limousine home halfway through a party. Unable to prize Diana off the dance floor, he abandons her to her young friends to party till dawn—the cause, on occasion, of rumors of marital discord, particularly after Diana's performance at the marriage of the Marquis of Worcester to actress Tracy Ward. The princess devoted most of her attention to handsome stockbroker Philip Dunne, whose energy and appetite for dancing clearly matched hers. The other guests' eyebrows rose; Diana's frenetic, nonstop dancing was described as "an extraordinary mixture of fist-punching in the air, and twisting down to the floor." As another guest remarked, "It's not the way you expect to see the future queen behaving." But, insiders tell me, Diana simply regards dancing as the perfect opportunity to let her hair down and burn off some excess energy. Her favorite dance tracks include Billy Joel's "Uptown Girl," "Beat It" and "Billie Jean" by Michael Jackson, Chris de Burgh's "Lady in Red," and Mick Jagger singing "Dancing in the Street." Put one of those on the turntable, and there's no stopping her.

So proud is Diana of her ability on the dance floor that, for a present to celebrate their wedding anniversary in 1988, she gave Charles a videotape of herself dancing to a version of "All I Ask of You," from her all-time favorite show, *The Phantom of the Opera.* As she gets to the end of the song—and her dance routine—she does a spectacular high kick, throwing her head back, perfectly poised on one leg. Then she twirls to face the camera with her arms outstretched and mouths the lyrics, "Say you need me now and always. Say you love me, that's all I ask of you." Charles had very mixed feelings when he received the gift. It did, after all, make a change from cashmere sweaters and Hermès ties. But he was also anxious—unnecessarily as it turned out—that a copy of the tape could fall into the wrong hands.

In fact, Diana's display of flirty dancing didn't come as a shock to Charles. Three years earlier, midway through a fund-raising show at the Royal Opera House in Covent Garden, a slender blonde appeared onstage with British dance star Wayne Sleep. (In fact, it's rumored to have been the diminutive Mr. Sleep who helped Diana stage the wedding-anniversary video.) To the great surprise of the audience—not to mention her speechless husband—the blonde was the Princess of Wales, revealingly clad (and braless) in a form-fitting gold silk dress. According to Mr. Sleep, "It was all her idea. For her, the excitement of doing it was to keep it from her husband more than anything else." They decided on "Uptown Girl," and rehearsed together at Kensington Palace. "She has rhythm, she can do high kicks, and she has a real feel for jazz dancing, which was great." On the night of the fund-raiser Diana slipped away from her husband and the other guests in the royal box almost unnoticed—only to appear onstage a few minutes later, and perform a routine that included everything from classical steps to the Charleston. The crowd went into a frenzy, although Charles is said still to cringe at the memory.

Most recently, inspired by the hit show *Tango Argentino* in London, Diana's signed up for private tango lessons, reportedly impressing her tutors with the ease with which she's picked up complicated dance steps. Perhaps she's hoping against hope that Charles will join her in the dance—it takes two to tango, after all. But, with or without her reluctant husband, we're unlikely to be treated to a public performance of Diana doing the tango. These days, she wisely keeps a lower profile, although she's more fitness-crazy than ever. Almost every morning begins with a dip in the pool; long before her sons are awake, Diana slips into a scarlet track suit, dashes to her car, drives the mile or so to Buckingham

Palace, and completes thirty fast laps of the pool there. She's frustrated by the fact that there's no space for a pool at Kensington Palace and is delighted, on weekends, to be able to stroll down to the heated indoor pool at Highgrove, the couple's country retreat, without having to dress first.

At Buckingham Palace, she always showers and washes her hair, waiting until she is back at home to style it (or have it styled) for the day. She uses The Body Shop banana shampoo and conditioner or, occasionally, a conditioner called Shimmer Lights, which keeps her frosting from turning green. But her favorite pastime often puts Diana under time pressure, and indeed, she was once stopped for speeding on her way back to K.P. after a swim. She was doing 55 m.p.h. in a 30 m.p.h. zone. Rumors flew. What could she possibly have been doing out at that time in the morning? She must have been returning from an assignation! But those who know that Diana relies on her early-morning swim to boost her energy level for the day ahead knew better. In fact, when Buckingham Palace's pool is being cleaned, and during renovations a couple of years back, she insisted on keeping up her habit, diving into the pool at the luxurious Berkeley Hotel roof-level health club. In a swimming cap, without a scrap of makeup, she passed unrecognized by most of her groggy fellow swimmers.

A few years back, Diana threw herself into tennis with a vengeance. She signed up for lessons at the exclusive $700-a-year Vanderbilt Racquet Club, in London's Shepherd's Bush. Conveniently, Harry's school is on the way to the Vanderbilt, and Diana can often be seen dashing down the steps of the Wetherby Prep School in her tennis whites and sneakers, flashing those devastating legs, on her way to a game. Her favorite partner in private games is Diana Donovan, who's married to the famous London photographer Terence Donovan. But she has played in public, to raise money for Birthright, a pet charity. She's said to be good, and getting better all the time, although Martina Navratilova needn't start looking over her shoulder yet. But give Diana time, perhaps; after the Wimbledon tournament a couple of years back, Diana asked Steffi Graf to give some lessons not only to her, but to her two sons. If she's got time after a session on the Vanderbilt court, she's also been known to slip into a regular exercise class there—where, I'm told, "she seems to lap up the glances she inevitably attracts, while pretending not to notice that she's the center of attention. But she's certainly the envy of everyone there, without an inch of spare flesh on her perfect body."

Diana is the first royal ever to sign up for public exercise classes. In October 1990, she tried to join another club, outside London, where she hoped to join in regular classes, without the press catching on. Using the pseudonym Sally Hastings, she worked out in the gym for an hour under the watchful eyes of exercise teacher Carolan Brown. But needless to say, as Diana has learned to her cost, there is no such thing as privacy when you are the Princess of Wales. By the following day, her presence was headline news, and Diana realized the impossibility of slipping in and out of a health club unnoticed. The club returned her membership fee. But Diana asked Carolan to consider becoming her personal trainer—and now Miss Brown puts the princess through her paces at K.P. for one hour, twice a week. Her usual fee is about $70 an hour, and it's believed that's what Diana pays.

Carolan's technique, called the Step, needs only one piece of equipment, a bench. The exercises are based on the usual aerobic workout, but involve continuous stepping on and off the Step. As Carolan says, "The good thing about it is that you can't cheat—you're either on it or off it! The foot patterns are simple, there's no dancing, and the exercise is constant." It burns the same amount of energy as running at seven m.p.h., "and because you're always using the thigh and buttock muscles, it burns 30 percent more fat than regular aerobics." So that explains Diana's perfect derrière. In fact, though, Diana's behind isn't her prime figure concern; after Harry was born, she was rushed off her feet and didn't follow her postnatal exercise routine. As a result, her stomach muscles are slacker than she'd like—and she has to work hard on them. When pictures of her in a bikini on King Juan Carlos's yacht appeared, she was crushed by rumors—sparked off by her rounded belly—that she was expecting again, when actually she'd never quite managed to get her abdomen pancake-flat after Harry's birth. Even now, Diana is dissatisfied with her body: surprisingly, she doesn't like her legs, either, and yearns for a bigger bust!

Even on vacation, Diana hates to let her regime slip. On tour in Brazil, she slipped into the pool of her Rio hotel for an early-morning dip, wearing a stunning pink-and-blue neoprene swimsuit. (Psychologists have actually expressed fears that she could be a victim of exercise addiction, a complaint common to fitness-obsessed young women who feel their world will fall apart if they so much as skip a class or a session of laps.) In fact, Diana feels that the one way she can cope with being cloistered with Charles's family—for instance, during the Christmas vacation at Sandringham—is to escape for a few hours to a nearby spa. Her minders—as many as three at a time—accompany the princess when she drives the seven miles to nearby King's Lynn, waiting while she spends forty-five minutes swimming, followed by a session lifting weights. She always emerges with a grin, refreshed and ready to face the family again.

Diana usually grabs this opportunity while the Windsors are out horseback riding. At the age of nine, she was thrown from her pony, Romany, and although as an adult she has taken up riding again so that she can accompany her pony-crazy sons, she has never quite conquered her fear of horses. Since her in-laws all share a passion for horses—her husband is a top polo player, her sister-in-law scooped an Olympic riding medal, her father-in-law, Prince Philip, loves carriage racing, and the Queen sometimes seems welded to her saddle—this fear has made Diana something of an outcast. For a while, she made the effort and joined them on horseback outings, but now prefers to reserve that time for the keep-fit pursuits of *her* choice. These days, an increasingly confident Diana is less concerned about what Prince Charles's family thinks of her.

The slender Diana is delighted to discover that a passion for exercise enables her to eat exactly what she pleases. But on two occasions since she met Prince Charles—just before her wedding, and again after Prince Harry's birth—Diana grew so thin as to inspire worries that she might have become anorexic, as her older sister Sarah once did. She was never seen eating in public—in fact, she finds public dining embarrassing and prefers to have a meal before she goes out—and slipped to a size 8, which is definitely too slender for a woman of her height. In time, Diana's weight stabilized. In the beginning, however, it was love that helped her shed the excess pounds—love for her prince, and anxiety about her upcoming nuptials. Thanks to the butterflies she felt in her tummy whenever she thought about the ceremony (or about her prince), steering clear of the calories was no problem.

Nowadays, she never has to watch what she eats and can indulge whenever she pleases. Diana hasn't shaken off a passion for chocolate; paparazzi who like to spend their weekends waiting for Diana to emerge from Highgrove have frequently caught her in flagrante as she emerges from the nearby candy store, laden with bars of Cadbury's chocolate and her favorite Kit-Kats. (She keeps them on hand for blood-sugar lows and declares that they give her instant energy.)

But aside from her chocoholism, Diana has embraced healthy eating, under her husband's influence. She never drinks, and the couple is virtually vegetarian; Diana will just occasionally indulge in a little fish or chicken. But she prefers a baked potato and salad; quiche Lorraine; hearty soups—all concocted by her cooks from produce grown in Prince Charles's own kitchen garden at Highgrove and delivered to Kensington Palace. Her favorite dessert is fresh fruit, and Charles can provide her with delicious peaches, plums, apples, and strawberries to her heart's content. The prince is Britain's best-known organic gardener, and Diana is also known to feel passionately that the couple and their children should avoid additives, pesticides, and herbicides in their food whenever possible. She once recalled her horror at discovering, on the label of a bottle of soda pop that William was guzzling, a long list of additives. From that day on, she banned all but the most natural of drinks and foods from her kitchen. A bonus: She has discovered that without their veil of potentially health-damaging chemicals, homegrown produce tastes better, too.

Staying healthy is Diana's number one priority. She

knows that a good diet and exercise are her greatest allies in the energy stakes, fueling her for the ceaseless carousel of private and public commitments. But diet and exercise aren't always enough. Quite high-strung by nature, Diana also resorts to aromatherapy massage— her favorite remedy to combat the stressful life. A friend recommened that she try a visit to Aromatherapy Associates in Fulham (a couple of miles from her London home)—and Diana was soon hooked. In fact, she so enjoyed her pampering sessions in the peaceful cream-and-blue treatment rooms that she suggested her sister-in-law, Sarah, should try the place out.

Aromatherapy—a fragrant massage using essential oils distilled from precious plants, herbs, and flowers— is an ancient art, but the princess has found that it works superbly to soothe away modern-day angst and tension. Because it is a therapy—albeit an "alternative" one— Diana had to begin her treatment with an in-depth consultation, going over her medical history and life-style, so that the appropriate treatment could be mapped out. Aromatherapy body massages can be tailored for different purposes: to energize, to banish stress, to induce restful sleep. Diana often has an aromatherapy treatment last thing during the day, if she has an evening free of official engagements, enjoying a blend of oils featuring vetiver and camomile, to guarantee a good night's sleep. If her appointment is in the morning, perhaps before an official lunch or a tough afternoon of official duties, the massage will be more invigorating, featuring oils containing rosewood, bergamot, and geranium. So effective has Diana found aromatherapy that although she often drives herself to appointments, it's always the chauffeur who ferries her home. This is for safety's sake: She's sometimes so wound down that she falls asleep on the backseat.

Diana likes to use aromatherapy products at home, between treatments, too. Diana (and Fergie) have both fallen for Daniele Ryman's aromatherapy skin-care oils and unguents, concocted to their own specifications. For stress, Diana adores Ryman's bath-time oil, which boasts basil, camomile, and melissa. For insomnia, the princess will dab a few drops of orange and neroli on her pillow sham. Even the rooms at Kensington Palace are more fragrant these days, thanks to "environmental scents"— perfumes that invigorate or relax the atmosphere—supplied by Ryman. "Fragrance should be inhaled—it can change the mood, and how one feels," declares Ryman. Many members of the Royal Family, including Diana, now travel with Ryman's jet lag kits, featuring Asleep and Awake oils—which live up to their names, making it easier to adjust to new time zones.

In fact, like other members of the Royal Family, Diana is a great believer in alternative medicine. When she has a minor health worry, she doesn't ring her M.D.—she's likely to summon her acupuncturist or a homeopath. Homeopathy is championed by the Royal Family: nobody has quite come up with a satisfactory explanation for *how* this therapy works, but its devotees swear by it. It involves taking tiny amounts of compounds—found in nature and bound with glucose for palatability—and dissolving them on the tongue, several times a day.

Diana also indulges in Joseph Corvo's Zone Therapy—in fact, she's been visiting this Yorkshire-born royal favorite since she was fifteen, when her grandmother Lady Fermoy introduced her to him. Far more than a beauty treatment, Corvo's technique focuses on the electromagnetic currents that supposedly course through the body. Zone Therapy is based on the theory that the body is divided into ten different zones—five on the left, five on the right. Corvo claims that as a side effect of contemporary living, we eat, drink, and breathe toxic substances, which form crystalline deposits in the nerve endings of these zones. High-pressure massage of corresponding points in the hands and feet can help to break the toxins down, enabling the body's energy to flow more freely. Almost any health problem can be tackled, from asthma to circulation problems, arthritis to obesity—indeed, Corvo is alleged to have helped Diana shed over thirty pounds, following the birth of her children. Diana, like other members of her family, is a firm believer in Zone Therapy even though, as anyone who's experienced it (or, some say, endured it) will admit, it's sometimes painful. And if it sounds as though Diana does nothing but go for salon visits or lie back and be pampered, that's far of the mark; she evenly spaces her therapies and beauty treats, rarely indulging more than once a week.

Certainly, to look at Diana, she appears the perfect English rose; her slavish devotion to health pays off. But that rosy English complexion can have its own problem: oversensitivity. A longtime fan of The Body Shop and its environmentally friendly cosmetics whose packages can be refilled to reduce waste, Diana has been known to send her bottles to Kensington High Street's branch of the shop for refills. She swears by their Peppermint Foot Lotion and keeps a bottle in her limousine for between-appointment massages, to keep her feet cool and un-puffy. This is made easier by the fact that as soon as the sun comes out, Diana abandons pantyhose. She uses a fake tanning product on her slender legs until nature does the trick for her.

She has also, in the last few years, added products by the French beauty company Clarins and America's Erno Laszlo to her bathroom shelf. Like thousands of wealthy women all over the world (for Laszlo products are anything but cheap), Diana is now a member of the Erno Laszlo Institute, with her own membership card.

She gets her products from longtime favorite store Harvey Nichols, which she visited personally for her first consultation, and now goes through her twice-daily Laszlo regime religiously, knowing that she can't afford to have a breakout mar her complexion. Prince Charles has laughed about her obsession with the Black Sea mud soap that's integral to the deep-cleaning routine, but Diana knows that it works for her; she follows up with a ritual thirty splashes of warm water, as prescribed.

About once a month, Diana books in at the exclusive Janet Filderman salon for a facial. She first visited just before the birth of Prince William, when piling on the pounds had left her feeling below par. The one-hour luxury treatment kicks off with makeup removal, using delicately perfumed Milk of Roses cleanser. This is swiftly followed by Bright and Clean, a freshening toner. The skin is then sterilized with an ozone machine, and pores (which Diana finds get clogged by London's dirty air and the makeup she must wear) are deep-cleaned with a "skin vacuum." This is followed by a calming fifteen-minute massage.

One reason Diana always looks so fantastic is that she never lets herself get stuck in a time warp, even when a particular look works for her. She has switched hairdressers several times, and as a result, her hairstyle has been constantly updated (not least because each new coiffeur wants to make his or her mark on the princess). To begin with there was Kevin Shanley of the salon Headlines, who transformed Diana's natural hair color—rather mousy—into a glimmering gold with subtle frosting. He also banished Diana's bangs, showing her the wisdom of taking her hair back off her forehead to show off her fabulous bone structure and noble brow.

There was a falling-out, over a swept-up hairstyle that the press declared a "Di-saster," and Diana took up with Richard Dalton, Kevin Shanley's partner in Headlines. (Shanley's relationship with Diana went from frosting to frostiness when he later sold secrets of life inside Kensington Palace to the tabloids.) Dalton, too, now seems to have been given the royal brush-off, and Diana has two hairdressers: Scots-born Sam McKnight (who is also the man responsible for transforming supermodel Linda Evangelista into a blonde), and Ivor, of the Carey Temple McAdam salon. (Salon partner Denice McAdam is already familiar with royal patronage: It was she who created the Duchess of York's stunning wedding-day ringlets, and tended her locks for some time afterward.)

Diana worked with Sam McKnight on perhaps her most stunning photo op to date: the session with *Vogue* photographer Patrick Demarchelier, which once and for all confirmed her status as one of the world's great beauties. Much in demand as a magazine stylist, McKnight is often away on exotic trips; hence Diana's visits to Ivor at Carey Temple McAdam, for trims. Gregarious McKnight is clearly a royal favorite, however; after he had styled her hair for a Kensington Palace dinner party, Diana is reported to have invited him to join her guests at the table.

It's taken time, but Diana has worked hard to find the perfect look for her extraordinary life-style—and the balance of exercise and diet that enables her to deal with being a mother and a career woman, working for a public that expects its princesses to look nothing less than exquisite.

# 6

# Princess of Work

These days, one word is used time and again to describe Diana: caring. During more than a decade of official duties, Diana has realized that, far from being a mere figurehead, she can actively improve the lives of those who are less blessed than she is. While her family will always come first, Diana is now utterly devoted to her work as a "career royal." And as a result, she has become an extraordinary asset to what Prince Charles's grandfather, George VI, used to refer to as the family firm.

What makes Diana different is her willingness to reach out to others—literally. Although protocol dictates that royals must never be touched publicly, apart from brisk handshakes, Diana often makes the first affectionate move. She never shies away from physical contact with the old, the infirm, or the very young; she's always willing to cuddle a child infected with HIV, stroke a sick person's back, or cup a pensioner's face in her hand. In olden times, it was actually believed that monarchs had miraculous powers and could cure certain illnesses simply by touching the victims. And while Diana certainly doesn't claim to be able to heal the sick, others aren't so certain.

The family of car crash victim Dean Woodward, for instance, insists that it was Diana who helped the twenty-four-year-old emerge from a coma. When Diana first encounterd Dean, he was on a life-support system in the same Nottingham hospital where Prince Charles had undergone surgery for the serious polo injury to his right arm. Diana took time off from visiting her husband to tour the thousand-bed hospital. When she came across Dean, she sat on his bed, holding his hand and urging him back to consciousness.

Some months later, to Diana's glee, Dean had made a full recovery. With alacrity, she took the Woodwards up on their offer to visit them in their modest semi-detached house, where she was introduced to Dean's two small children, and met his fiancée, Jane Fisher, again. Expressing her joy at Dean's renewed health, she later even wrote the kind of warmhearted thank-you note a person might expect from an old family friend. "This comes with my love to you both and my heartfelt thanks for making me feel so welcome today—I left your home full of special memories." The signature was "Lots of love, Diana"—and only the Kensington Palace address gave away the fact that this intimate missive was from the future Queen of England.

On another occasion, the bemused mother of Beirut hostage Terry Waite was puzzled to receive a birthday bouquet out of the blue. "Who do we know called Diana, living in Kensington?" Mrs. Waite asked her family. Although she had a million other things to think about, Diana had spared a thought for the seventy-six-year-old woman who, she knew, would be sad to be separated from her beloved son on what should have been a joyous day.

In the past, while undertaking a punishing schedule of engagements, the royals have very much been figureheads: snipping ribbons, planting trees, declaring open everything from museums to housing estates. Charities lucky enough to lure royal patronage have their fortunes assured. For some reason, people believe that "royal" charities must have more integrity, must be worthier than others—or maybe they feel there is more cachet in giving to a fund headed by a member of the U.K.'s first family.

Diana, though, is very much more than a ribbon-cutter. In order to empathize with the problems of the deaf, for instance—she is patron of the British Deaf Association—she mastered sign language. Many charities of which she is patron speak of her ongoing behind-the-scenes interest in their work or research. She asks them to load her up with "homework" so that she can establish the best way in which to help, and really understand the problem they are dealing with—whether it's combating an often-fatal illness, finding shelter for the homeless, or helping couples iron out their differences.

Since Diana sometimes has four or five official engagements a day, the homework can be intense. Waiting for her in the Jaguar limousine that carries her from appointment to appointment is a pile of files for last-minute review: relevant clippings, brief biographies of dignitaries she's going to meet, financial reports. She hates to let anyone down and once turned up at a banquet at the Savoy while in the throes of a painful stomach bug. (She didn't touch a morsel.) Her devoted dad, for one, isn't convinced that his daughter's heavy workload is a good thing. The earl—who was himself a royal equerry, to King George VI—declared, "In my day, the royals only had to do one job a day. My Diana sometimes does two or three or more. She loves it, but I am worried that she is working too hard."

In the case of the marriage-counseling charity Relate, with which Diana has an especially close relationship, she has actually sat in as a passive observer during therapy sessions. One wonders how much couples could pour their hearts out with the Princess of Wales breathing down their necks! It's said that Diana has a special affinity for Relate because of the rocky patches in her own marriage that she and Prince Charles have weathered.

The princess now has more than forty carefully chosen patronages and is anxious not to take on too many; she has to feel certain that she can give each one her all. A palace source reveals: "When the Princess of Wales accepts a patronage, she involves herself completely and works very hard. When she goes to their engagements she meets the organizers she already knows, questions them, and builds up relationships. Her interest is genuine. She wants to know exactly what is going on; she finds out how she can help—and then does so. She spends as much time on her patronages as she can possibly slot into her official program. She is a diligent, caring, self-motivated person who always keeps appointments."

Eccentric British TV personality Sir Jimmy Savile, a man who has himself raised millions for charity, recalls the time he asked Diana to take part in a TV special entitled *Drugwatch*. "I thought she might like to take part because she is a parent," he recalls. "And when I contacted her, she just said, 'Oh, great. Wow!' I would have no hesitation asking for her help again. She has this very special rapport with handicapped people. It has nothing to do with being a princess. It's simply that she is a very lovely person. And when she visits handicapped people, something really like magic happens. People who feel low seem to cheer up when this beautiful lady chats to them."

Despite the challenge of combining a career with motherhood, Diana has an incredibly heavy workload. During 1990, for instance, she crammed in an astonishing 323 official engagements. "Operations Centre" is a suite of rooms (tastefully decorated with duck-egg blue walls and raw silk curtains), in St. James's Palace; Diana likes to keep her team separate from the royal H.Q., which is nearby Buckingham Palace, her mother-in-law's home. Endless invitations and requests for patronage come in. Her itinerary is mapped out months in advance, at twice-yearly meetings. Before Diana says yes to anything, her staff check the diary—and check again, to make sure the event doesn't clash with a school concert or a son's birthday. But these days, Diana juggles her diary to ensure that she does the maximum work possible. Disco Di, the girl who seemed self-obsessed and more interested in her social life and shopping than her official duties, has become Dutiful Di.

As Prince Charles predicted (in not terribly articulate fashion) before their wedding, "I think that as Diana begins to do various things . . . that very often, you get many more invitations, you meet more people, you suddenly find areas of things that you think, 'My goodness, I must . . . I'd like to do something about improving things here or encouraging there.' "

Where Diana has really worked miracles is in breaking down fears surrounding certain frightening illnesses. Take Hansen's disease, better known as leprosy; not once, but twice, on overseas tours—to Indonesia and northern Nigeria—she paid visits to leper colonies. For centuries, people had feared that if they came near lepers—let alone touched them—they would catch the dread disease. But in Nigeria, at the Molai leprosy hospital, an ungloved Diana—with her customary care and sensitivity—reached out and held the hand of one of the patients. The signal she sent to the world was clear: "Don't shut these people out. They need care, and love, and attention, just like anyone else. And if I can touch them, then there's no damned reason for *you* not to."

She seems to take particular joy in banishing prejudice. Another case in point is her visits to people with AIDS, which occur with ever-increasing frequency. During a solo visit to the United States while Charles was recovering from his polo accident, Diana kept a date to visit a refuge for children with AIDS. When a cute little three-year-old—abandoned at the center when she was just ten months old—asked Diana, "Can I have a ride in your car?" the princess didn't hesitate for a second, but scooped the overjoyed child into her arms and kept her on her lap while the chauffeur drove the Rolls-Royce around the block.

In the U.K., she has often been photographed with AIDS patients—and, as always doesn't just chat to them, or listen, but touches them, too. Declares one AIDS charity worker, "Gestures like that do more to counteract ignorance and irrational fear about AIDS than millions of pounds' worth of advertising." Now Diana's gone so far as to become patron of the National AIDS Trust, too. Since the princess showed her willingness to have everyday physical contact with AIDS patients, she has sparked a shift in public attitude—with the result that in many cases, certainly in the U.K., those afflicted by

Young Diana Spencer in the carefree days before her parents' acrimonious split.

*(Globe Photos)*

Wearing her diamond and emerald necklace Hiawatha-style, the trendsetting Princess enjoys a rare twirl with her reluctant dance-partner husband during a 1985 Australian tour.
*(Globe Photos)*

Did they let her win? Fit and fast on her feet, Diana finishes first in the annual sport's day race for mothers at William's school.
*(Rex Features/The Sun/Terry Richards)*

Diana is pictured with Princess Grace of Monaco at her debut public engagement. Here Shy Di wears the daring, low-cut black taffeta dress for the first, and last, time.

*(Globe Photos)*

Diana takes a seat alongside the Queen Mother, who helped mold the young Lady Diana into a regal princess.

*(Globe Photos)*

Diana and Charles share a few words with the family's precious "Granny," Queen Elizabeth, at the annual Epsom Derby horse race.

*(Globe Photos)*

Still young and very much in love, Diana's face shows the pride she feels at producing her husband's son and heir—and Britain's future king.

*(Globe Photos)*

Soon after his easy birth, the devoted mother shows her newborn Prince Harry to the cameras.

*(Globe Photos)*

Diana's affectionate nature shows whenever she's around children, especially her own little Princes.

*(Rex Features)*

There's nothing the Princess likes more than a good cuddle. Her sons—unlike their father, who was rarely hugged as a child—are used to public displays of affection from devoted Diana.

*(Rex Features)*

The Queen wanted Prince William to stay home during Charles and Diana's first Australian trip, but they wouldn't have missed his first steps for the world.

*(Globe Photos)*

Diana lifts three-year-old Harry up to get a better view of the cheering crowds during the festive annual Trooping of the Colour ceremony.

*(Globe Photos)*

The Prince of Wales takes a beautiful bride—Diana's greatest day, if not her greatest choice of gown.

*(P. Lichfield/Camera Press/Globe Photos)*

Showing off her extravagant engagement ring, Charles and Di hug for the cameras during the rehearsal for the wedding of the century.

*(Snowdon/Camera Press/ Globe Photos)*

In 1988, before rumors of a rift began to surface, Charles lays a protective arm on Diana's shoulder—or at least, her shoulder pads!

*(Globe Photos)*

At a gala benefit for the London City
Ballet, one of her favorite causes, Diana
accepts one of dozens of bouquets she's
given every day.

*(Randy Bauer/Ron Galella Ltd.)*

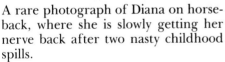

A rare photograph of Diana on horseback, where she is slowly getting her
nerve back after two nasty childhood
spills.

*(Jim Bennett/Camera Press/Globe Photos)*

Diana does New York. Her whirlwind
tour included a visit to a homeless set-
tlement, where she earned applause
for cuddling an H.I.V.-positive baby.

*(Ron Galella)*

Becoming more beautiful and regal by the year, Diana manages to keep still for an official portrait.

*(Globe Photos)*

Gone are the designer gowns when Diana becomes "one of the boys" for a visit to an oil rig.

*(Globe Photos)*

Stunningly dressed in black, a color she's usually forbidden to wear except when in mourning, Diana arrives at the Vatican for a private audience with the Pope.

*(Globe Photos)*

On the slopes and having fun before the tragic avalanche that killed the Prince of Wales's friend and nearly killed the Prince himself.

*(Globe Photos)*

The world's most photo-
graphed woman never fails
with a smile for the cam-
eras.

*(Globe Photos)*

Diana's baby isn't a baby any
more—the Prince and Prin-
cess of Wales deliver Prince
Harry on his first day at
school.

*(Globe Photos)*

Stunning in a black and white evening gown by her favorite designer, Catherine Walker.
*(Camera Press/Globe Photos)*

Diana and Charles en route to another Royal Wedding, Andrew and Sarah's, in which the Princess played a vital matchmaking role.
*(Globe Photos)*

A kiss for her sweaty, polo-playing Prince, before his devastating fall.

*(Globe Photos)*

In happier times, Charles and Diana ski together. Now, she takes her sons, while Charles stays home.

*(Globe Photos)*

A pensive moment during yet another grueling royal tour of Australia.

The tug-of-love Spencer children—Diana and her brother
Charles, who's had his own share of marital ups and downs.

*(Globe Photos)*

the virus do not also have to bear the burden of being outcasts. Elsewhere, when she talks to the mentally handicapped or physically disabled, she is deliberately giving a blessing to members of the community whom others find hardest to face.

As Roger Singleton of the Barnardo's Children's Homes observes, "Some people find it very difficult to confront people who are seriously disabled. It's something that she takes on board in a very direct and open way. She knows that if she spends time with handicapped children, parents are watching her to look at her reaction. If she will accept their children, then that helps them to feel that the rest of the world might. I've heard parents say, 'If my kid's good enough for the Princess of Wales, she ought to be good enough for everyone else.' It is very uplifting for them."

She is certainly famous for her affinity with children, whom she draws to herself like a magnet. If they want a cuddle, who cares about royal protocol? Diana's only too pleased to have a little affectionate contact herself. During one Australian visit, while separated from her sons by 13,000 miles, Diana visited a Sydney kindergarten and stayed far longer than planned, admitting that "it's heaven to be back among children again." Remembering her experience communicating with small children during her stint as a teacher, she readily squats for a one-to-one at *their* level, to ensure that they aren't intimidated by talking to a woman who is both tall *and* a real-life princess.

Visiting sick children in the hospital, Diana has trouble tearing herself away from their bedsides. Such visits often distress her. While presenting the Children of Achievement awards for youngsters who have overcome physical disabilities, Diana admitted—after watching little Lynsey Jephcott shuffle forward painfully on her walker to collect her medal—that "I am an emotional wreck on occasions like this."

Wherever she goes, her genuine caring is appreciated. Those she meets are left with the real feeling that she cares and understands their plight. That isn't always the case with royals; the Queen, for instance, can often seem remote and removed from her loyal subjects' problems. These days, Diana is often being compared to the Queen Mother, Prince Charles's grandmother, who is famous for her care and compassion.

It's almost as if Diana has vowed that, to somehow repay her debts for the privilege and wealth that fate bestowed on her, she must do as much for the under-privileged as she can manage. In just one day, she spent an hour and a half visiting with terminally ill patients at St. Joseph's Hospice in East London. Later that night, at Prince William's instigation (evidently he has inherited his mother's warm heart and thoughtfulness), Diana visited homeless people and chatted with them for over an hour and a half. As one down-and-out twenty-five-year-old, quite overcome with emotion, explained afterward, "It's almost impossible to describe how much meeting the princess means to me. That someone like her should care enough to leave Kensington Palace to see me and all these other people who have nothing . . . I thought there was no one who gave a damn. It has restored my faith in people."

The princess is absolutely determined to hack her own path through the jungle of charities, good causes, and social issues. But she knows there's a handsome payoff, too: Her excellent public image (an invaluable boost to the Royal Family's dwindling popularity) means that in other areas of her life—such as choosing where her sons go to school, how to raise them, or where to holiday—her mother-in-law will take a backseat and let her have her way.

The fact is that Diana—who doesn't have a single academic credit to her aristocratic name—is quite simply brilliant with people. And if you were going to be queen one day, it is a skill you might dream of being blessed with. It is all the more extraordinary that she manages to come across as being so utterly natural when you consider what an extraordinary event any visit from the POW really is. She is preceded by the police, with their sniffer dogs. These are swiftly followed by the palace staff, her own security staff, the press corps—and more police, for good measure. Yet, amid this throng, Diana manages to convey a sense of intimacy with each and every person she stops to chat with on her now famous "walkabouts."

A walkabout is a security guard's nightmare—and fears for the princess's safety in this most vulnerable of situations have proved well founded; on at least one occasion, a member of the crowd has lurched forward and attempted to grab the princess. Security must by necessity be intense; in fact, it has been stepped up ever since a kidnap attempt on Princess Anne was foiled some years ago. But Diana, above all the other royals, has proved her determination to mingle with the people wherever possible. If it causes headaches for her minders—well, that's too bad. According to one observer of Diana's walkabouts, "She never just goes down to the front. If there's someone at the back who might be a bit shy, she will seek out that person—not in a way to make them feel even worse, but she will talk to them and make them feel good about themselves." Another enchanted veteran of a POW encounter relates: "When she disappears out of sight again, it's as if, somehow, a light has gone out."

Hands-on Diana breaks another royal rule, too: She sometimes even signs autographs. While visiting a home for abused children, Diana gave one little boy a message to treasure; she signed herself "with lots of love and a big hug."

Despite the fact that she finds public speaking agonizing—she hates what she regards as the "plumminess" of her voice—Diana has learned to deal with her fear. It once seemed almost as if she were deliberately avoiding any kind of public appearance that required her to do anything more than smile and look stunning for the cameras. But Diana has always been impressed by how her husband's speeches on subjects like architecture, organic farming, alternative medicine, and ecology can sway public opinion. She took coaching and now writes many of her own speeches—she finds it easier to remember things when she has written or rewritten them herself. Outsiders are now impressed with the authoritative air of Diana's public speaking.

She does usually manage to throw in a *joke* or two, often at her own expense. When she was ceremonially presented with the Freedom of the City of London, for instance, soon after the tabloids had come up with the particularly outrageous allegation that she had begun to hit the bottle, Diana smiled and declared: "Contrary to recent reports in some of our more sensational Sunday newspapers, I have not been drinking and I am not, I can assure you, about to become an alcoholic." Despite the fact that she admits to being "terrified" before opening her mouth in public, Diana relies instead on some deep yogic breaths.

Another vital element of the princess's work is her

overseas tours—at her husband's side, or increasingly, solo. The Queen is head of the Commonwealth, a group of nations that includes Australia, New Zealand, Canada, and some far-flung parts of Africa. Member nations clamor for a visit from the Queen, her children, or their glamorous consorts. Since Britain is part of the European Community, there are plenty of short-haul hops there, too, boosting trade and good relations between the countries.

What might appear to be the most glamorous element of Diana's duties, though, is actually the most arduous. Royal tours have been described (fairly accurately) as "1 percent glamour and 99 percent hard work." Beneath the flag-waving, red-carpeted razzmatazz is a grind that the public rarely gets to see. As an exhausted Diana herself recalled, back in the U.K. after her very first overseas tour to Australia in 1983, "The first week was a shock. It was like a baptism by fire, but having got into the feeling of it, it got better. By the time I left Australia, I felt I'd actually been able to achieve something. But people tend to think that if you're going to Australia or New Zealand, it's a holiday, but actually, it's our busiest time, much busier than over here."

The royals' staff dread overseas tours, which are almost literally military operations. Getting the royal show on the road is no breeze. Planning takes months—and packing almost as long. Much as Diana might love to step nonchalantly aboard a Concorde with a change of clothes in her hand baggage, life as a royal isn't that simple. On one Australian tour in particular, Diana had cause to be grateful that, by traveling on planes from the Queen's Flight, she avoids a bill for excess baggage: Reportedly, the royal couple arrived with no fewer than ninety pieces of baggage (which included fifty-five pounds of William's diapers). Every meteorological and social eventuality is catered to, with each item meticulously folded, labeled, and catalogued before being loaded into Diana's knockproof custom-made aluminum suitcases and trunks. Diana never travels without a leotard, a bikini, and a tennis racquet. Nowadays, since she rarely travels on business with her sons, her staff make sure to slip silver-framed photographs of them into her baggage instead; the photos appear by her bedside during each new stopover, as if by magic. She likes to take her own creature comforts, too; for an official visit to Rio de Janeiro, Diana's staff made sure her favorite decaffeinated Nescafé instant coffee was packed—even though she was visiting the coffee capital of the world.

The royal retinue can run to a dozen staff: ladies-in-waiting, equerries, private secretaries, dressers, hairdressers. Diana has so far drawn the line at taking her personal trainer. There are two doctors, too, who travel with a full medical kit: sterile hypodermics, (royal) blood plasma (these items are particularly vital now that AIDS has become a worldwide scourge), anti-allergy drugs, antibiotics—everything, in fact, that might be required to contend with a full-scale emergency. The doctors take turns on duty, but mercifully, their services are almost never called upon.

Diana does, however, suffer jet lag. On board the plane, she follows all the rules: She puts her feet up (with a pile of homework, rather than the Barbara Cartland or Danielle Steel book she'd love to escape into), drinks nothing but pints of mineral water, and eats only lightly; she also travels with soothing and reviving aromatherapy oils. Her best piece of anti–jet lag advice actually came from *Saturday Night Fever* star John Travolta, who advised her to "sleep as much as possible, and exercise as soon as possible upon arrival." Diana follows that advice to the letter, but still—like even the most seasoned jet-setter—occasionally finds herself wiped out by traveling across time zones. While in Australia for the country's bicentennial bash, she confessed that she could remember nothing of the spectacular celebrations she and Charles had witnessed soon after their arrival a few days before. The festivities had included a stunning sail-past of tall ships and a rousing chorus of "Waltzing Matilda." Though in an exhausted daze, Diana had managed to smile throughout.

The princess has grown accustomed to the spotlight, but it never shines more brightly than when she's on tour. Her every Charles Jourdan–shod step is chronicled by the press corps who tail her around the globe. She has, by now, built up an easy, almost jokey relationship with them—and they adore and admire her for the ability to switch on a dazzling smile to order, which keeps their editors sweet and their own bank balances healthy. She teases these hardened newshounds about traipsing around the world on their expense accounts. And when one journalist insisted that it was hard work reporting on her tours, she grimaced and declared, "Oh, you make me want to cry. Where's my Kleenex?"

The press corps is, of course, on hand to capture Diana's most glamorous moments. There are star-studded encounters, like that White House ball when she opened the dancing, fox-trotting competently with an utterly bewitched John Travolta, before going on to meet Neil Diamond, Tom Selleck, and Clint Eastwood, who said afterward, "She made *my* day!" Diana laughed coquettishly and responded, "But I'm only twenty-four!"

These encounters are merely the icing on the cake, however. For every tango with Travolta, Diana must endure dozens of visits to widget factories, oil rigs, and old-folks' homes, not to mention operas, ballets, trade fairs, and fashion shows. At one Palm Beach ball, for instance, Diana found herself seated with a dozen doddery dignitaries, none of whom was under ninety. She has learned to make small talk with hundreds of strangers, making them feel at ease.

And as Harold Brooks-Baker observes, "I have seen both Diana and Charles at dinners where they have only been able to sit down for about thirty minutes during an entire evening. And they are plagued the whole time by people who don't know how to approach royalty, especially when they are abroad on tour."

Not every approach is entirely innocent, either. Once, during a visit to New York, a banner-wielding IRA supporter got too close to Fergie for comfort. Security is stricter than ever during overseas tours, probably because of host nations' paranoia that something terrible might befall a royal on their territory. At home, royals travel with just a couple of detectives, whose guns are discreetly tucked inside their tailored jackets. Abroad, entire platoons of minders are assigned to them, and bulletproof glass is routinely installed in public places they are to visit.

If Diana is secretly rattled by worries for her saftey, though, she is too much of a pro to let it show. Meanwhile, her hosts aren't taking any risks. During an American tour, for instance, Diana had only one scheduled opportunity to meet with real people, rather than bigwigs: a walkabout in a mall, following a visit to an exhibition called "The Best of British" at J. C. Penney's.

Shortly before she was due to arrive, a Secret Service man received a warning call saying that "something bad would happen" if the princess showed up. The security people immediately decided to cut the walkabout short, and when Diana—surrounded by no less than thirty-five special agents—walked over to greet the waiting crowds (some of whom had been standing for six hours to catch a glimpse of her), she was hustled into her Rolls-Royce and whisked to safety, treating thousands of disappointed people to a grandstand view of the agents' broad backs, and nothing else.

As on so many occasions, it turned out to be a false alarm. A flustered telephone operator had scrambled a message from an anonymous caller who'd actually said that something bad would happen to the princess's *image* if she was seen shopping in such an ordinary place. And so, Chinese whispers transformed a tip on taste into a full-scale security alert.

In her time, Diana has endured more than her fair share of criticism. It was said that she was shirking her royal duties, that she was obsessed with her social life, her stardom, her clothes—and she was duly picked apart as a result. But over the last few years, at home and away, she has made a concerted effort to set a very different example, with her own special touch. During the Gulf War, when royalty was criticized for neglecting the armed services (and the spouses who waited at home), Diana visited army bases in the U.K. and Europe and wrote a message of support in which she revealed that she, too, was following events in the Gulf hour by hour on TV and in the newspapers. Not only that, but she and Charles virtually abandoned their social life for the duration of hostilities, canceling private trips to the opera and other planned entertainments. The princess maintained that she would not be able to enjoy herself while the world was at war.

Diana has proved that she is very much more than a pretty face. And these days, she is leading a new fashion: for compassion. As a result, the world has taken her to its heart. And—with hugs, loving gestures, and hand-written notes—she has clearly taken the world to hers.

# 7

# Precious Moments

ome is where the heart is. And it's clear from the minute you walk inside the door that Diana's heart is in Highgrove House, her beautiful country home. *There* are little Wills's pristine gumboots; *there* are the immaculate garden tools, rinsed down after the merest poke in the dirt, *there* are Di's flower-collecting baskets. And off to the left is the gilt–and–eau-de-Nil living room, cozier and warmer than you'd find in many a country house, although lined with the requisite ancestral portraits. (Only these ancestors happen to be George III and Queen Charlotte.) Glossy coffee-table books jostle for surface space with geraniums in bone-china cachepots. There's a menagerie of dinky Herend animal mantelpiece ornaments; there are bronze statuettes of Prince Charles on his polo pony—and, for comfort, there are piles of kilim rug–covered cushions on the window seats in the large hall, ready for guests to take out onto the lawn, so that their rears don't get damp. In fact, whenever they're at Highgrove, Diana and Charles like to spend as much time in the fresh air as possible. French windows are flung open and meals are taken on the lawn—weather permitting.

Not surprisingly, whenever there's a chance, Charles and Diana leap inside his distinctive red helicopter and beat the traffic jams to be in Gloucestershire in little more than a few minutes. Kensington Palace is grand— and the Waleses' suite there belonged to generations of royal ancestors before Diana got her hands on it. But Highgrove is where Diana has created a real family home, away from the pressure and from prying eyes. In fact, what Diana has achieved at Highgrove is a triumph. She was decidedly unimpressed when Charles first proudly showed her around the sandstone house, which he had recently purchased from Maurice Macmillan (son of former British premier Harold Macmillan): Back then, Highgrove boasted just a few reject pieces of furniture from Buckingham Palace and was in need of a dramatic overhaul.

Diana acted fast—and with Charles off hunting, she put her time to good use, consulting with Dudley Poplak, a South African who's worked a lot for her mother. Diana is a real home-loving girl, a fact she always attributes to being a Cancerian. Charles had fallen in love with Highgrove's garden—or at least the *potential* of the 350 acres surrounding the house—and was happy that the interior should be Diana's territory. For over a year, the couple camped, moving from room to room, living with builders' rubble, and eating scrambled eggs while sitting on sofas covered in dustsheets. (They found it romantic to be just like any newlywed couple in a new home that needs work.)

At Highgrove, Charles and Diana can be normal. (Well, at least, they can *pretend* to be normal.) Wills and

Harry get their parents' undivided attention for a while, riding BMX bikes or ponies through the grounds. And Diana gets to let her hair down—or simply not wash it, for a change. Queen-to-be she is, but at heart Diana is just an ordinary housewife who delights in popping into the convenience store, jostling with other mums as she searches for bargains or picks out something special for William and Harry. In the nearby Cotswold market town of Tetbury, where Diana's been shopping for ten years, nobody bats an eyelid when she pops into the butcher, the baker, the candy store, or the pharmacy.

As one shop assistant in the local branch of the pharmacy chain Boots reveals, "She regularly shops here. She's always courteous and never afraid to ask about a product. And if there is something cheaper without the brand name, she'll buy it." Shopping without fanfare or special privileges is one way that Diana keeps her size 9's firmly planted on the ground—although, unlike most young moms, she's always tailed by private detectives. (If she does ever manage to escape their watchful gaze, there's a furor. During the 1990 Christmas holiday at Sandringham, Diana went for a long, solitary walk along a windswept beach, miles away from her minders. She splashed through seawater puddles with only hundreds of wading birds for company. A passerby said she appeared to be "totally absorbed in her innermost thoughts—she was obviously enjoying herself." A telephoto lens captured the princess's pensive expression—but a lone gunman would have had the same access, and the Queen was furious at her for taking the risk.)

Diana resists the red-carpet treatment whenever possible. A friend of mine was amazed to see her flipping through packets of pantyhose in Harvey Nichols alongside a dozen other women. And the manager of one

Kensington store declares, "She just walks in. We are not pre-warned and she never insists on any special treatment. She has lovely manners, not like some of the big stars. When Madonna came in here she insisted that the doors [be] closed. Of course, that drew a crowd and stopped the traffic." Diana feels that happens to her quite often enough in the course of her official duties. In her private time, she yearns to be treated just like you or me.

Diana—once Shopaholic Di—still loves to shop. But to the chagrin and disappointment of many a London merchant, she does it less now than she did a few years ago, when she was a fixture on the "Tiara Triangle," a corner of London turf that takes in Kensington and Knightsbridge, and was so called because Diana and Fergie were spotted almost daily, checking out the merchandise: costume jewelry from Butler & Wilson, lingerie from Janet Reger, cute toys from Frog Hollow for her sons. Her Jaguar was almost a fixture on London's "yellow lines" (no-parking zones); her chauffeur would wait in the car and watch for parking-meter wardens, while Diana's bodyguard followed her into the stores. These days, in fact, Diana seems to get almost as much of a kick out of picking up a sliced loaf and a couple of bunches of flowers as she did in the days when she'd return home to Kensington Palace laden with extravagant parcels.

The food at Highgrove is always simple, whether or not Diana's wearing her cook's hat: homemade soups, poached salmon, apple pie, salad, and fruit. Charles insists that as much food as possible should come from his organic garden, so the Highgrove cooks make do with whatever is in season. When there's a good crop, visiting friends have been known to go home with boxes of fresh organic fruits and vegetables (and the staff arrange a twice-weekly delivery to Kensington Palace). As the late oil magnate and philanthropist Armand Hammer once recalled, "When we were about to leave Highgrove, Prince Charles suddenly disappeared and returned to present us with several boxes of plump, sweet strawberries which he had picked himself. He was more delighted to give us berries he had grown, and picked with his own hands, than if they had been jewels from the family vaults." The oh-so-rich royals are all thrifty, though—and nothing must be wasted; bumper harvests go straight in the deep freezer.

Diana's greatest joy was when her indoor swimming pool—a wedding present from her father's estate workers at Althorp—was installed. She fell in love, too, with her dream German kitchen, another wedding present. Actually, Diana likes nothing better than to give her cooks (who have waited patiently all week for their mistress to arrive) the weekend off and prepare all the meals herself, including her sons' favorite bacon sandwiches. For Diana, home cooking's a relief after all that banquet food.

Classical music wafts out on the breeze, through the open French windows. Although Di earned a reputation for loving pop music, she insists that she prefers classical every time; she loves Mozart, Vivaldi, and Handel, and has become a real fan of opera. In London, she is a regular visitor at the Royal Opera House, where a box is set aside for her to entertain friends during intermission. In yet another attempt to be "one of the people," however, she prefers to join the jostling throng in the Crush Bar—a place that really lives up to its name. Declares an opera-loving friend who's found herself almost cheek-to-cheek with the princess on more than one occasion, "She likes to have a Perrier and a smoked salmon sandwich with everyone else, and listen to snatches of gossip. Personally, I think she's mad—it's a zoo, compared to her opulent box."

True, Charles and Diana share a love of music. But they couldn't be more different in their choice of spare-time activities. Charles's are mostly solitary: painting; gardening; reading works on philosophy, psychology, spirituality. Even on weekends, he has a heavy load of paperwork to plow through. Diana likes to settle down with a Judith Krantz best-seller, or to watch soap operas or "The Clothes Show" on TV—but mostly, she seeks out the company of her friends and family. In fact, it often seems as if only their sons bond Charles and Diana together.

For her boys, Diana is prepared to make sacrifices she never would for her husband. For example, Diana dislikes riding—there was that childhood accident I've mentioned—and made only halfhearted attempts at the sport in spite of Charles's desperate efforts to persuade her back into the saddle during the early years of their marriage. But when Harry and Will pleaded with her to join them they (and Major James Hewitt, a handsome riding instructor) succeeded where Prince Charles had failed.

Riding isn't the only sport that Diana has taken up for her sons' sake. She has also, in the last couple of years, been seen out shooting—a practice she used to protest against loudly on the grounds that it's barbaric. But organized parties to shoot pheasant and grouse are crucial elements in the aristo social whirl, and Diana put a brave face on her disgust and horror when William became old enough to join other male family members out shooting. Diana—dressed in a green Barbour oilskin coat and cocooned in warm sweaters—grudgingly joined in the festivity, keeping a sharp eye on her son. It may well be, in fact, that she chose to tag along simply to ensure that tearaway William stayed well away from the dangerous end of a gun barrel.

The Waleses not only have different leisure pursuits, they frequently holiday apart, too. Charles likes to fish, and as yet, his sons don't have the patience to join him. He finds their presence distracting when he's painting and prefers to disappear abroad for a few days with his watercolors and sketch pad, leaving Diana to hold the fort. But the young boys get their fair share of holidays— mostly with Mummy. Because of Charles's polo injury, he was advised not to join Diana for the boys' first foray to the slopes. He missed a treat. Diana took off with her sons to the exclusive Austrian resort of Lech, making up a party with close friend Catherine Soames and Charles's exuberant cousin, Viscount Linley. The resort was blissfully deserted, except for the usual pack of press photographers. As one skier commented, "The masses go to nearby St. Anton. This is not a place for anyone on a budget."

Diana hadn't skied since the 1988 Klosters avalanche tragedy, when the Waleses' close friend Major Hugh Lindsay was killed. On the bunny slopes, however, there was no danger for Harry and William, who had the time of their lives finding their ski legs. Harry, so often overshadowed by his important elder brother, outshone William this time. It's said that the earlier you learn to ski, the better you'll be—and certainly, Harry took to the sport like a duck to water, snowplowing through his instructor's legs within forty-eight hours. To his frustration, William was nursing a cold throughout the trip. On just his second morning, he had a coughing fit and burst into tears; Diana had to take him back to the chalet. But since the boys have shown real prowess, skiing looks set to become an annual event that they will look forward to all year long.

Diana's greatest frustration is that she cannot convince the press—and in particular, the paparazzi—to draw a line between her public duties and her private time. She feels very strongly that she works hard enough to earn the right to be left in peace when off duty. As if it weren't irritating enough to have every step dogged by watchful minders, there's almost always a photographer lurking in the wings, too. Matters came to a head in November 1987 when Jason Fraser, a twenty-two-year-old photographer, snapped Diana as she was leaving a private dinner party in a Kensington mews house, in the company of one of her favored "walkers," Major David Waterhouse. Supposedly, Fraser was backed up against a wall and threatened by the princess's private detective before the princess herself "burst into tears" and begged him to give up the film, which he duly did.

Money-grabbing photographers with two-way radios and motorbikes have frequently made Diana's off-duty life a misery; they have a detailed knowledge of Diana's habits, relentlessly pursuing her to her favorite restaurants and shops and the homes of friends and confidantes. And after more than a decade, Diana still finds their persistence harrowing. At the time of the Fraser incident, a member of the royal household declared: "It's becoming a war of persecution."

Small wonder, then, that Diana seeks out the seclusion of Highgrove at every possible opportunity. There, too, though, Charles has had to take steps to protect their privacy. A drystone wall surrounding the estate has been raised several feet, and the grounds are peppered with video cameras. It is a cause of some regret to the prince, who—pointing to a camera in a tree—told me, "It's a shame; no matter how well you disguise them, they still stick out like a sore thumb—but I suppose it's something that one has to live with." He has lately gone one stage further, banning all aircraft from flying lower than two thousand feet above Highgrove to ensure that no intruders can buzz his family's precious home. This measure was sparked by two incidents when aircraft chartered by tabloid newspapers came too close for comfort.

For most of the week, however, Diana is based at their London home, triplex apartments 8 and 9 in Kensington Palace. On some nights, her country-loving husband joins her there. But while Kensington may be a palace, Diana has tried to add the personal finishing touches that have transformed Highgrove House into a beautiful residence that would not only look good gracing the pages of any design magazine, but is a pleasure to live in, too.

Off leafy Millionaire's Row, where many embassies are found, Kensington Palace (worth a cool £500 million, according to real estate experts) has been likened to a royal village, with fourteen members of the Queen's family in permanent residence. There Diana and Charles do most of their formal entertaining. (Invitations to Highgrove are reserved for only the closest friends and family.) And although Diana started her princesshood shyly, barely opening her mouth for the entire duration of an evening and happy to let her knowledgeable husband sound off to his heart's content, it's a different story now. "Diana has developed into a stylish hostess—quite formidable, in fact," reveals one veteran of several K.P. dinner parties.

It's the most sought-after ticket in town. After checking (via an internal phone) that you're really on the guest list, an officer of the Royal Protection Squad ushers you through the security barrier. You go past a police post with several closed-circuit TVs and the Duke and Duchess of Gloucester's pad—number 12. Walk through the archway built by Christopher Wren (the architect who designed St. Paul's Cathedral, where Diana and Charles were married) and it's like stepping three hundred years back in time. The London traffic becomes a mere hum. An earlier visitor once called Kensington Palace "a romantic place of secret walled gardens, sunlit ponds, and cobbled courtyards." The gravel crunches beneath your feet as you walk across one of those gaslit courtyards toward the Waleses' immaculate black front door.

Of course, the door is opened by a butler, who takes your coat (if it isn't a warm evening—and it usually isn't). If you're a man, you're in a tux. For women, long dresses are usually safe—but nothing too flamboyant; the Princess of Style doesn't like being upstaged! The first thing that is likely to strike you is the decor. While homey, it's unquestionably royal: Prince of Wales feathers pattern the green-and-gray carpet. (Bob Geldof, an intimate of the prince's, once commented: "Don't think much of your carpet!" Prince Charles was forced to admit, "It is a bit garish, isn't it?")

A massive, exquisite portrait of Diana hangs alongside those of her royal predecessors; it was commissioned by Charles in 1984, when she excitedly told him she was expecting Harry. Charles decided that he wanted a portrait of Diana wearing her memorable Emanuel wedding dress, and the result—by Royal Academician John Ward—is stunningly beautiful. You glide past Diana's picture, then up the Georgian staircase to the first-floor drawing room and a much-needed drink of sherry or Bollinger champagne.

This is a warm, welcoming room in shades of honey. It was created by Diana in tandem with her first interior designer, Dudley Poplak, who also did much of the work at Highgrove. (She is said to have switched allegiance to Nicky Haslam, a favorite of rock stars like Bryan Ferry and Mick Jagger and adored by high society for his wit and flamboyance. He's just one of the regular guests you might find yourself sitting next to—Diana and Princess Margaret, her neighbor in Kensington Palace, seem to share him!)

The Waleses put care and thought into their guest lists, dividing people into groups: politics, art, and show business—and of course, a smattering of family. (Viscount Linley is a frequent guest.) Depending on which group you fall into, your dinner companions might be King Hussein and Queen Noor of Jordan, ex-king Constantine of Greece, Diana's fave designer, Catherine Walker, politicians Neil Kinnock and John Major, the Duke and Duchess of Westminster, Lord and Lady Tryon (she is Charles's friend Kanga), Placido Domingo, Kiri te Kanawa. (At times, such world opera greats have been called on to provide the after-dinner entertainment!) The whole of *Who's Who* seems to have been to dinner at K.P. at some time or other. And Diana takes it all in her stride, knowing that she's more famous than any of her guests.

When everyone's arrived (and hardly anybody dares to be late), guests follow Diana into her dining room, often marveling out loud at the flowers. She has recently given the Royal Warrant to her favorite florists, Harper & Tom's in nearby Notting Hill, who fill the house with their exquisite informal arrangements. She loves highly scented flowers, and the dinner table will often have full-blown roses in low vases, which look magnificent in the candlelight Diana prefers.

Although the table can be extended to seat thirty-six, Diana and Charles think ten guests is ideal, so that they can have a proper chance to talk to everyone. Knowing full well that everyone's likely to be a little bit twitchy, Charles has a ritual to relax everyone: soon after sitting down, he'll turn to a neighbor and say, "Pass the bloody salt, will you?" Everyone laughs, and the ice is broken. Smokers, though, may find the evening torturous. More than one has been discovered sneaking a surreptitious cigarette in the garden; Diana and Charles are fervently antismoking, and ban tobacco from their homes. (In Diana's study, there's a large NO SMOKING sign.)

Guests needn't fear a horrendously rich meal. The table setting—with its Brierley crystal, George III silver, and gold-and-green Spode china—is generally more exotic than dinner itself; the Waleses like to eat lightly, and are proud to provide most of the ingredients themselves. Free-range chickens, game (from the royal estates), and plenty of fish feature on the menu. Charles's particular favorite is Aylesbury duck, and though he may stick to vegetarian dishes when he's eating alone, he indulges in meat-eating when there are carnivorous guests around. To begin with, there's almost certainly soup—watercress, or perhaps sorrel or nettle, made by the K.P. chefs from Charles's own recipe. There are always dishes and dishes of seasonal organic vegetables, often driven up from the Highgrove kitchen garden that morning to ensure their freshness. Dessert will be light: a mango sorbet, a raspberry fool, or just occasionally chocolate ice cream. In keeping with tradition, the ladies leave the table first, and then the port is passed around.

Charles and Diana set the place cards themselves. She sometimes frets about where to seat the more attractive women. Apparently, during one such crisis of placement, she was somewhat reassured by her butler, who simply declared, "Ma'am, you could put her on the prince's lap and it wouldn't matter. At the end of dinner, she will go out of the door and you will still be here."

During the years after her marriage, of course, Diana played the part of a Lady Who Lunches to perfection. She shopped till she dropped in the Tiara Triangle, often meeting close friends for long, gossipy lunches at one of her favorite restaurants. Now that Diana has thrown off her frivolous image, however, those outings are few and far between—but all the more precious.

When Diana does eat out, however, she's as much a star spotter as the rest of us. Her long-time favorite restaurant is San Lorenzo in Beauchamp Place, where Diana was first spotted having a tête-à-tête with Charles's old flame, dress designer Lady Kanga Tryon, six years ago. It's accrued even more special memories since a highly self-confident Prince William booked a table to take his mother there for lunch before he went off to boarding school. Diana is also a regular at Le Caprice, where she's even been spotted wearing shorts and a leopard-print top!

Diana has, of course, never paid much heed to royal protocol. As a friend comments, "She's just a touchy-feely sort of girl." And lately, Diana's joined the "mwah, mwah" brigade of double cheek-kissers, too. The affectionate greeting isn't just reserved for close friends. The welcoming, Italian-mama proprietor of San Lorenzo, Mara Berni, exchanges kisses with Diana as she ushers her to a table where the princess can watch celebrities like Jack Nicholson, Robert Redford, and Lauren Bacall tucking into the restaurant's legendary crudités, pasta, and cream-filled pancakes. Until she married into Britain's first family, the closest Diana got to movie stars was having their photos on her wall—and despite the fact that she's met so many of the world's luminaries now, Diana is still attracted by all the glamour.

Generally, Diana sticks to restaurants that are a gemstone's throw from Kensington Palace. Particular favorites are the two owned by Simon Slater and Nick Smallwood, Launceston Place and its noisier sister, Kensington Place. (When she wants to dish, Diana goes to Kensington Place; the din made by diners is so loud that it drowns out conversation for everyone but your chosen lunching companion.) More sedate—and a real mecca for the Ladies Who Lunch (especially Sarah Ferguson)— is chic Harry's Bar, in Mayfair, where it's members only.

Wherever she goes, though, Diana still has her "tail," the bodyguards who ring up in advance to secure two tables, so that they're constantly on hand. Their presence is known to get to her at times. On occasion, Diana has reportedly been spotted driving through town in the wee hours of the morning—in an attempt, perhaps, to clear her head and get away from it all.

But Diana has grown to love her London home, even though she felt quite out of place there at the start of her marriage. As Charles spends more and more time at Highgrove, in his beloved countryside, she has felt more and more as though London is *her* territory. In fact, she likes nothing better—on those oh-so-rare occasions when there's nothing in the diary—to slump in front of the TV in her private sitting room, tune into a soap opera like "Eastenders," which she's known to love, slap on a moisturizing Clarins face pack, and be as much of a couch potato as you or I. At times, she must reflect on how life hasn't quite turned out the way she planned it. But then, it's unlikely that anyone but a naïve virgin would have taken on the task she so gladly volunteered for.

Diana probably never anticipated, for instance, that she would often wind up sleeping in a separate room from the prince of her dreams—but that's the way the royals have always lived. In fact, her own father sleeps separately from her stepmother—and they're still besotted with each other! Diana sleeps in a massive (seven-foot-six-inch) four-poster bed that Charles had transferred from Buckingham Palace when they were first married—and on which, incongruously, are placed her and Charles's stuffed animals. (She's a sucker for furry frogs—an in-joke reference to the fact she "kissed a prince—and he turned into a frog!" Charles has a threadbare teddy that has been around the world with him several times.)

Quite often Charles will camp on a bed in his dressing room. There will be no early-morning snuggles for the royal duo. Prince Charles explains that it's a decision "arrived at for purely practical reasons. Diana and I have such busy schedules that if we shared a room, we would only get under each other's feet." And when you've an itinerary like Charles and Diana's, every second of sleep is precious.

It's hardly surprising that since Diana has to live so much of her life in the limelight, she likes to have a few secrets. For instance, she befriended a disc jockey at the London music station Capital Radio, and likes nothing more than to have tunes cryptically dedicated to her over the airwaves. The songs are often middle-of-the-road numbers by Neil Diamond or Billy Joel, which she listens to as she prepares for the day ahead. DJ Graham Dene reveals that "I often play records for her and send messages in code. I once played 'Uptown Girl' and said, 'This is for Charlie's angel in the red bow tie,' because when we met once she was wearing one. Every time I play 'Uptown Girl,' I give her a mention. It's almost become an expected thing between us."

Dene recalls that, in return, the princess has invited him and his mother to Kensington Palace, and on one occasion the princess put through a personal call to him on his birthday. Initially, he refused to believe it was really her. "Princess Diana got through to reception and was apparently quite rude. The engineer said the princess was on the phone to me; I thought it was one of the secretaries and kept saying to her, 'Lovely joke, nice try.' But the princess kept saying, 'No, Graham, it really *is* me.' She was amazingly lovely and patient and just wanted to say 'Happy Birthday' and have a chat with me. The next year she did it again. Here's a person with thousands of engagements and an incredibly full life, and she remembers my birthday!"

But Diana has what's described as a "special touch," and Dene's revelations will come as no surprise to those who know her intimately. She never forgets a friend's birthday—or their child's. She likes to shop for gifts personally, rather than dispatch an equerry or a lady-in-waiting, snapping up Christmas gifts months in advance because of her tight schedule. For birthdays and Christmas, close friends don't just get the official Wales portrait (usually a photo of the four of them); they're likely to receive a jokey card, too, perhaps even one that pokes fun at the royals and their tired old rules.

In fact, declares an insider, "Diana strives constantly to be the girl next door. She craves a normal life more than anything, now that the glamour has palled. It's impossible, of course—because she's surrounded by a phalanx of security men, reporters, and photographers—not to mention royal groupies. On the one hand, Diana loves the glory of her role—but she'd like to switch it off at will. The tragedy of her life is that she can't. Like Greta Garbo, Diana just wants to be left alone. And who can blame her?"

# 8

# The Little Princes

*D*iana only ever had one ambition: to be a mother. That may sound outmoded in this day and age, when the world of careers is a woman's oyster, but Diana still believes that motherhood is the most important job of all for a woman—and her husband agrees. In fact, the only job that Diana truly enjoyed before her marriage was her last position: as a teacher on the staff of the Young England school, a Montessori kindergarten, where she would gladly spend all day bending down to chat eye-to-eye with her young charges, indulging in messy games or getting up to her elbows in fingerpaints.

She has a way with children. And for her two young boys, born into a world of privilege and pressure, there could not be a better woman to ensure that they grow up unspoiled, unselfish, and caring, able to withstand the perils of drugs, alcohol, and indolence that send so many young aristobrats spinning off the rails these days.

If Diana was a picture of happiness on her wedding

day, then she was positively bursting with joy when, just two and a half months later, she took a pregnancy test and discovered that she was expecting a little prince or princess. Diana knew full well that it was her duty to become pregnant as quickly as possible—she had, after all, been chosen specifically for the task of providing the future King of England with heirs—but even *she* was surprised by how quickly it happened. The resentment and embarrassment caused by her prenuptial gynecological exam were completely forgotten when she did, so soon afterward, become pregnant.

Initially, pregnancy didn't quite turn out to be the blissful experience Diana had always dreamed of: She suffered hideous morning sickness that often extended around the clock, and, having slimmed down for her wedding, resented having to trade her new designer clothes for billowing tents so soon afterward. "I feel just like an elephant," Diana complained.

On June 21, 1982, at 9:03 P.M., Diana gave birth to one of the most important babies in the world: William Arthur Philip Louis (to be known as Prince William of Wales, but soon nicknamed "Wills the Wombat" by his dad). Prince Charles was on hand to experience every contraction, whispering words of encouragement and endearment. "I think it's a very good thing for a husband to be with a mother when she is expecting a baby," he had told crowds at the beginning of Diana's pregnancy. But that, in itself, was a major break with royal tradition: Until Prince William's birth, royal fathers had paced up and down the palace corridors. (In fact, earlier royal births took place in the presence of the home secretary, a government official, who had been required to witness royal births ever since the occasion when James II's wife reputedly switched her stillborn baby for a healthy infant, smuggled into the Queen's boudoir in a warming pan).

The Queen had naturally assumed that her eldest son's eldest child would be born, in line with centuries of tradition, at Buckingham Palace. But Diana was highly nervous that something might go wrong and implored Sir George Pinker, the gynecologist she shares with the Queen, to explain to her mother-in-law the importance of a hospital birth. In the end, a bed was booked at the Lindo Wing, a private sector of St. Mary's Hospital, Paddington, where royalty and rock stars alike await their new arrivals. The Lindo Wing may lack the gilt and grandeur of Kensington Palace—rooms lack private bathrooms and are outfitted with purely functional furniture and garish floral wallpaper—but Diana didn't care; she preferred to think that she was in the safest of hands if the birth didn't go smoothly.

Diana had prepared for her big day with natural-childbirth classes given by Betty Parsons, a septuagenarian whose no-nonsense approach to having a baby has helped literally thousands of aristocratic women through the experience. (Titled London mothers are now devastated that Mrs. Parsons has retired. But she will almost certainly be on the job if the princess adds to her family in the future.) In the event, Mrs. Parsons herself was on hand to take Diana through her breathing exercises— "Doggy, doggy, candle, candle" (pant, pant, blow, blow)—soon after Diana checked into the Lindo Wing with Prince Charles at five in the afternoon. In the end, the agony grew too much for this first-timer to bear: She opted for an epidural anesthetic, an injection that numbs from the waist down.

Prince Charles's bliss at having a son and heir was clear to the loyal crowds and photographers gathered on the doorstep outside the Lindo Wing; he had never looked so happy. He paused to chat briefly with the waiting press before driving home to a bottle of chilled champagne and a small family celebration. When asked if the new baby—who weighed in at seven pounds, one ounce—looked like his father, Prince Charles grinned. "Fortunately, no."

Diana couldn't wait to take her son home. Less than twenty-four hours after the birth—a very brief stay for a first-time mother—she emerged from the hospital with her tightly wrapped princely bundle. But she was definitely looking less than radiant. Diana was horrified later, when she saw the pictures of herself outside the Lindo Wing, wearing a green maternity dress, carrying a lot of excess weight, with her hair looking slept-in—this, on what should have been her proudest day. She learned her lesson: When Prince Harry was born just a couple of years later, she ordered a slim-line red suit and booked an appointment for her hairdresser to visit the hospital before she checked out.

Diana's motto for motherhood has been "I'll do it *my* way." Royal mothers were not expected to breast-feed their children; that would conflict with their duties. Diana vowed that *her* children were going to get all the health advantages of breast-feeding, which helps a baby's immune system by passing on antibodies through the milk. If she did have to leave William, she expressed milk so that he could be bottle-fed with it.

Both Diana and Charles were raised in upper-class households where children were seen and not heard; their nurseries were far from their parents, whom they generally only saw at appointed hours. Although William and Harry have their own top-story nursery wing in Kensington Palace, Diana wanted her children to be very much part of daily life. (Indeed, now that they are growing up, and there are fewer fears of chocolaty finger marks on the upholstery, there are no longer any areas out of bounds to the boys.) Both Diana and Charles vowed that their children were going to have "as normal a life as possible." The nanny they employed—forty-two-year-old Barbara Barnes—was to help with, not to take over, child care. And Diana found that she actually enjoyed changing her baby's diapers and bathing him. Even Prince Charles took his turn.

There was a period of marital readjustment, as usual after a new baby arrives on the scene. Diana so fell in love with her first born that for a while Charles felt edged out and neglected. His wife, for her part, suffered dreadful postnatal depression, which as a side effect robbed her of her usually voracious appetite. Diana lost vast amounts of weight, prompting Prince Charles to consult top doctors, who assured him that it was nothing serious: She was simply exhausted. Nanny Barbara Barnes stepped in, offering to take on more responsibility for William's care, but Diana insisted, "A mother's arms are so much more comforting. William comes first . . . always."

The thought of being separated from her baby for a long period of time was quite horrifying to Diana, even though she realized that she would soon have to take up her royal duties again. Her "maternity leave" was drawing to its close; an Australian tour was looming. But again, daring Diana broke the rules: She asked if young William could go along. Six weeks away from her son, at a time when every day there are new developments to delight a mother, would have broken Diana's heart.

Understanding the stress Diana had been under—the wedding, followed so soon by the birth; the adjustment to life eternally in the spotlight—the Queen gave her blessing, which thrilled both William's parents *and* the Australian people. But Diana soon realized that taking her nine-month-old son abroad was a mammoth undertaking. William arrived in Australia with almost more baggage than his parents: disposable diapers, lightweight clothing, special foods, and multivitamins. It had been decided that William would be based at a large, comfortable house in the small town of Woomargama, and whenever they had a breather in their schedule, Diana and Charles would dash to his side. William took his first teetering steps while they were in Australia. It was a moment Diana wouldn't have missed for the world, let alone for her mother-in-law.

To Diana, the whole episode had been a great success. The royal household had other recollections of the experiment, which had been a logistical nightmare. The royal entourage had filled thirty-three rooms of a hotel and four bedrooms of the house at Woomargama. So two months later, when Charles and Diana flew off on a tour of Canada, William stayed at home with Nanny Barnes. Diana would ring twice a day to talk to her baby, even though he could do little more than blow bubbles at her over the phone. She put a brave face on things but, when celebrating her twenty-second birthday during the Canadian trip, admitted that "my perfect birthday present is going home. I can't wait to see William."

Diana and Charles always planned to have more than one child: an heir and a spare. Indeed, two sons were an essential "insurance policy," in the unthinkable event that anything should happen to William (as it so nearly did in 1991, when William suffered a fractured skull at his boarding school in a freak accident with a golf club). So, having reestablished their former closeness some time after William's birth, the couple found their happiness made complete by the discovery that Diana was pregnant again. She was delighted that William would have a little royal playmate—and hopeful, too, that a younger brother might help keep the boisterous boy out of mischief. William's parents, and his nanny, had already discovered to their cost that you couldn't leave the boy unattended for a moment. He had developed a penchant for flushing his father's custom-made brogues down the toilet, and on one occasion (unable to resist the temptation to push a button on the wall, while nobody was watching him) had accidentally summoned the police to Balmoral. Diana nicknamed him "my mini-tornado," but beamed with pride at her fast-developing son's playful personality.

Throughout her pregnancy with Harry, Diana was once again plagued by morning sickness and lethargy—although this time she was careful to watch her diet closely; she had vowed not to put on so much weight. But feeling below par didn't keep Diana (who was becoming the consummate professional) from working right through her pregnancy. In fact, just the day before delivery, her duties included (appropriately enough) declaring open The Birthright Centre for mothers and babies, at London's King's College Hospital.

A little over twenty-four hours later, everything went like clockwork when Prince Henry Charles Albert David—to be known to one and all as Harry—made his way into the world, at four twenty P.M. on Saturday, September 15, 1984. Again, Diana had opted for the Lindo Wing; again, her husband was on hand to support her—but this time around things went so smoothly he even fell asleep at one point during the proceedings! The morning after the birth, Nanny Barnes brought

William—who by then was just over two years old—to the hospital to greet his little brother. Diana was relieved and delighted when Wills fell instantly for the little red-headed baby; she had been fearful he'd throw a jealous tantrum. In fact, it was love at first sight: At the photo session set up by Prince Charles's celebrated photographer uncle, Lord Snowdon, to mark Harry's christening a few weeks later, William carefully balanced the infant on his knees and gave the camera his proudest smile.

Harry settled happily into the nursery suite alongside his brother. And Prince Charles, then allegedly searching for new meaning in his life, decided to throw himself into fatherhood with gusto. For almost the first year of Harry's life, Charles's diary was a near blank, as the prince played with his son, bathed him, changed his diapers. Before William's birth, he had read countless baby-care books—but with the arrival of Harry, he decided to put them into practice. Charles had been fond of children ever since the age of twelve, when—to everyone's surprise, and delight—the Queen presented him and his sister, Princess Anne, with two brothers. Charles was so enraptured that he sat down and wrote for Prince Andrew and Prince Edward a most charming children's tale, *The Old Man of Lochnagar,* which he expertly illustrated with watercolors. (The book was later turned into a stage play, and there are now rumors that it may be filmed.) With this story-weaving skill, it was often Prince Charles who confected bedtime stores for his small sons' delight. And Harry seems to have benefited from his father's omnipresence; he is certainly a quiet, thoughtful, and affectionate child. (Rumor has it, however, that Prince Charles's goofing off from royal duties to spend valuable time with his second son sparked a major row with his disciplinarian father, Prince Philip, who was furious that his son had carried out just twelve public engagements in a four-month period.)

Actually, Charles is rarely openly affectionate with his sons. But Diana couldn't be more different. At every opportunity, even in public, she ruffles their hair and cuddles them—yet somehow, she's managed the delicate juggling act of mothering without smothering. When Diana isn't working she still heads straight for the idyllic surroundings of the heirs' nursery suite, tucked away beneath the eaves at Kensington Palace, with sloping ceilings and views of London's rooftops; the three particularly like to stare out at the kite flyers who have for decades flown their kites over Kensington Gardens' Round Pond. William and Harry's rooms are a world of adventure—but while they're spacious, a stranger would never guess that they belong to two of the richest children in the world.

There is a room, with miniature desks and chairs, for homework. Diana often comes there to supervise the boys; she's often incongruously dressed in an evening gown, because she has to leave for an engagement. The boys sleep in another room, which they share; during the school year, Harry has complained to his mother of occasional loneliness, now that his big brother's away at school.

Harry is the shy one; William is more gregarious and outgoing. William went through quite a difficult phase— he was sometimes described as "brattish" and once threatened his classmates at Mrs. Mynor's kindergarten by saying he would "send my knights to kill you when I'm king."

In fact, Diana was once heard to lament to her cousin by marriage, Austrian-born Princess Michael of Kent (who lives near the Waleses in apartments at Kensington

Palace): "How is it your children are so good, while mine are such a pair of tearaways?" But their misdemeanors have mostly been minor. Harry's worst crime seems to have been blowing raspberries at reporters. Compared to the behavior of most energetic young boys, the little princes' is—well, just plain average.

Diana adores them both, but nevertheless is relieved that her sons have now come through their wild babyhoods. Diana's initial instinct, when employing a woman to care for her sons, had been to steer clear of the starchy, brusque, uniformed sort of nanny who likes to reign over a nursery—the type of nanny she and Prince Charles had experienced. But perhaps she went too far in the other direction, because in 1987, the boys' first nanny, Barbara Barnes, resigned amid rumors that she'd been too soft and indulgent with the little princes.

Her replacement, Ruth Wallace, is a former nurse. Before taking charge of William and Harry, she worked in the radiotherapy and emergency rooms at St. Bartholomew's Hospital in London and had enjoyed a stint in the employ of ex-king Constantine of Greece. Her care and compassion toward children impressed Diana when she first encountered "Roof," as the children affectionately call her. Diana offered her a job that no nanny in her right mind would refuse. She is assisted by Olga Powell, a lady in her early sixties who's been "on the Wales team" since William was born.

Diana, Charles, Ruth, and Olga have worked together to mold the two boys into well-behaved young royals who can be a credit to their parents and their country. Prince William, in particular, must be prepared for the task of reigning over the United Kingdom one day, and must learn to grasp the importance of the role carved out for a boy who will one day be king. Prince Charles once poignantly described this as "something that dawns on you with the most ghastly, inexorable sense. I didn't suddenly wake up in my pram and say, 'Yippee!' Slowly, you get the idea that you have a certain duty and responsibility, and I think it's better that way, rather than somebody suddenly telling you."

From the moment William and Harry were born, they have been making public appearances—waving to massed crowds on the balcony at Buckingham Palace, making occasional church visits on Sunday. They have learned to smile and be polite while accompanying their parents on duty—even when they'd rather be playing at home with a train set, or riding their ponies. Ever since they were old enough to toddle, the boys have been learning to shake the hands of dignitaries, VIPs, and commoners alike, showing off perfect manners—in public, at least. (In private, it may be a different matter: Diana admits they can still be "little devils" sometimes. She adds that "when they are, they get a whack where they feel it!" Nanny Roof is also permitted to administer a short, sharp smack; bottom-whopping offenses include teasing animals, interfering with someone else's property, and—the most heinous sin of all—rudeness.)

By five, William appeared to be developing into the perfect gentleman. At the age of three, he had already mastered the distinctive Windsor wave. (His father once confessed that when *he* was small, he truly believed the world to be a heavenly place: Whenever he left his home, people smiled and waved, overflowing with goodwill. Naturally, the small boy waved back. "I thought people were like that with everyone," he has recalled, revealing that touching early naïveté. "It wasn't until I was older that I realized all the warmth and affection was not for me, but just because I was a royal.") The day Prince

William started at the Wetherby School, Diana boasted to a group of retirees: "He is already opening doors for ladies and he's calling the men sir." But it is Prince Charles who's the strict disciplinarian. Just a stern gaze toward his children in public is enough to make them toe the line, whereas Diana has a tendency to collapse in a fit of giggles when her sons are naughty. Charles believes in deprivation as a punishment and an incentive for future good behavior. In 1987, Prince William, who had been bossy with a guardsman at Balmoral, was banned from the excitement of the Braemar Games "until he learns to behave himself."

It has been the Windsor way to expose young royals to the public as little as possible until their manners have been perfected; in fact, Prince Charles himself was a terrific fidget, and his grandmother would quietly lead him from church at the first hint of twitching or inattentiveness. The Braemar event caused a temporary rift between Charles and the more softhearted Diana, though; during the games they sat apart, Diana very obviously leaving a William-sized space between them to make her point. William apparently cried his heart out at home—but perhaps the lesson worked; he has not been spotted tormenting guardsmen since.

The royal security staff help with the "molding" procedure. For safety's sake, they sit in class with their charges and have been known to tell them off for misbehaving in front of their schoolteacher. Wills earned the nickname "Basher" at school and is reported to have pulled rank with a school friend once, declaring, "My daddy can beat up your daddy. My daddy is a real prince," before his bodyguard stepped in to point out that this wasn't a particularly regal way to behave. With a police-force background, most of the minders have a natural authority the boys respond to, although occasionally it brings out the worst in Wills and Harry, as it did in their father before them. "Making the policemen run" is a game that has been passed down from royal generation to generation.

The choice of schools for the young princes was the subject of long, thoughtful discussions between Diana and Charles. In the U.K., competition for places in the top schools is so hot that parents must register their children *at birth*—although it's doubtful anyone would dare turn Diana and Charles down, even if they left their choice till the last minute.

Mrs. Mynor's up-market nursery school was an obvious choice for the first stage in the princes' education; it is near Kensington Place, and the basement classrooms could be easily fitted with the bulletproof glass essential for a prince's safety in a country not infrequently the object of Irish or Arab terrorist attack. (If you believe that nobody would dare harm the royals, it must not be forgotten that Prince Charles's favorite uncle and mentor, Lord Mountbatten, was blown up by the IRA on his yacht, almost breaking the prince's heart.)

William and Harry each joined the school on turning three and spent two years there, enjoying the unpressured atmosphere, painting, learning to count, playing dress-up, and (expressing themselves creatively) pretending they are trees. Like most mothers, Diana felt highly sentimental the day she, Charles, and William (reveling in his role as knowledgeable elder brother) first took Harry to school. Charles, too, was moved. "It made me very sad," recalled the prince. "I had a bit of a lump in my throat when we left him."

When aristocratic children reach the tender age of five, however, more serious preparation for elite education must begin. Both Harry and William wore the smart gray-and-red uniforms of the Wetherby Preparatory School, two minutes' drive from Kensington Palace. To Diana, the proximity is essential. She likes to organize her working life so that she can visit the school as often as possible, and is spotted, most days, dashing up the steps to collect her beloved Harry. Events in the school calendar—the Christmas play, sports day, and holidays are clearly marked in her diary before any other engagements, to avoid clash. On sports day, Diana regularly throws off her heels, hitches up her skirt, and goes for the gold in the annual mothers' race, but to judge by recent performance (last year she came in fourth), her cup-winning form's behind her.

At school, the boys' quite different personalities have been revealed. William proved himself to be full of energy and highly intelligent. He is often the ringleader for boisterous playground games. Harry is a more sensitive, reserved, and creative child, who at first was too shy even to put his hand up to ask the teacher if he could visit the bathroom. But he soon showed a strong artistic and musical streak (both boys were enrolled for "Fun with Music" lessons at an early age). In fact, Harry twice stole the show in the Wetherby School's annual Christmas show, in 1989 as a goblin (though he may never forgive his parents for allowing him to be photographed by the press in his ridiculous elf costume) and the following year as a soloist, performing the enchanting carol "How Do We Get to Bethlehem?"

Diana acknowledges, "William and Harry are so different. Where William is confident and forthright, Harry is quieter and likes to watch everyone." Although it was William who took his mother for a celebratory lunch when she finally settled on a prep school, Diana has an extra-special bond with Harry; she is publicly extremely demonstrative with him—touching his shoulder, straightening his tie. William's birth was dynastic duty; Harry's birth was more a matter of choice. Diana knows that Harry will in some ways have a more difficult life; while William is being groomed to be king, Harry must always be the also-ran. It is hard for *any* boy to escape his older brother's shadow—but especially so when that brother will one day reign over a nation. A few years ago, when Harry had to have an emergency hernia operation, it was Diana who kept an all-night vigil at his bedside, while Prince Charles continued with a painting holiday in Italy.

Diana and Harry can further deepen their loving relationship now that William is at Ludgrove boarding school. Pain was clearly etched on both his parents' faces the day they had to say good-bye to their elder son at Ludgrove, knowing it was yet another milestone on the road to maturity; his parents have said privately that they can't believe how their sons' childhoods seem to be speeding by. Harry will follow William to Ludgrove Preparatory in due course, but meanwhile, the younger boy is torn between pangs of loneliness and enjoyment of the fact that his somewhat bossy older sibling is removed from the scene. Diana overflowed with pride when, in the summer of 1991, she had to present Harry with his first gymkhana prizes, for winning competitive events on his pony. Harry shows all the signs of being as fine a horseman as his father.

In time, the boys will probably go on to public school together—although Diana and Charles are known to have quite differing views about which school that should be. Diana favors the highly academic Eton, where her brother and many of the men in her social circle studied; it is less than a mile from Windsor Castle and would make frequent visits to her beloved boys a possibility. Charles, meanwhile, has his heart set on their following in his footsteps (and their grandfather Prince Philip's) to Gordonstoun, a Spartan Scottish public school where there is an emphasis on the great outdoors, cold showers, and macho pursuits. In the past, the education of a future king has been a matter for discussion between no lesser figures than the sovereign, the Archbishop of Canterbury, and the prime minister. But with William, Diana is likely to get her way. Unlike royal mothers before her, she has stood up bravely to the disapproval of the palace's old guard when it comes to how she raises her sons. She believes at all times that Mother knows best, and she is clearly being proven right.

Diana still yearns for William's company, even though he's enrolled as a weekly boarder and thus is able to visit Highgrove for weekends (though laden with a schoolbag full of homework). But she manages to resist the urge to spoil her sons. Candy, carbonated drinks, and chocolates are for special occasions only. She doesn't lavish endless toys on them, either, although they get plenty of gifts from well-wishers. (Many of these are passed on to underprivileged children, but some, such as the exquisitely painted rocking horse that was a gift from Nancy Reagan, find their way into the nurseries at K.P. and Highgrove.) The boys' idea of a great outing is still to go to the toy store Frog Hollow near their London home. Cuddly toys have now given way to train sets, model cars, and toy soldiers, and with a bit of pocket money, they stock up on plastic tarantulas or plastic flies suspended in fake ice cubes for playing a joke on Papa. In a material sense, William and Harry are far less jaded and blasé than many of their contemporaries; in London, it is not difficult to encounter affluent, world-weary six-year-olds who seem to have been everywhere and done everything and are bored by life.

While she can restrict her spending on toys, Diana finds it much harder to deny herself the pleasure of dressing her sons in clothes fit for a prince. Until the Princess of Wales arrived on the scene, royal children had been dressed in the most conventional style: velvet-collared overcoats and short trousers in sensible country colors—which Diana can't stand; she hates muddy shades. These now make up only a fraction of the boys' more formal wardrobe. Instead, Diana favors Continental styling, mixing knee-length red shorts with an exquisitely cut brass-buttoned blazer, for instance, worn with knee-high dark socks in the French style. The princes usually wear loafers, rather than lace-up brogues. The labels Lacoste and Chipie feature heavily in the boys' wardrobes. On one occasion, Diana asked Catherine Walker to make for her sons beautiful pale-blue wool coats to match her own.

The princess will often dress her sons almost the same, putting them in identical (but different-colored) T-shirts or sweatshirts. The same tones don't suit both boys; William has Diana's fair coloring (which tans easily), while Harry inherited the Spencer family's freckles and red hair. He burns easily; on holiday, Diana slathers him in high-SPF sunscreen.

Certain old-fashioned courtiers may mutter in disapproval when they see the future King of England and his brother lounging around in sweatpants and sneakers, but Diana realizes that to join in the rough-and-tumble games that boys of their age so enjoy, her sons need a closet full of sweatshirts, Oshkosh dungarees, Benetton sweaters, jeans, and sneakers. It saves a fortune, she reasons, on dry-cleaning!

And who do they play with? Who makes up the royal tea set? Diana is anxious to keep her children away from ambitious, social-climbing parents who might be tempted to exploit their relationship with the royal household. Luckily, the boys were born with plenty of cousins. Peter and the tomboyish Zara Phillips (Princess Anne's children) are frequent weekend visitors to Highgrove, little more than a stone's throw from their own country home, Gatcombe Park. Lady Rose Windsor, daughter of the Queen's cousin the Duke of Gloucester, is another regular guest. But the most frequent visitors are Alexander and William, the children of Diana's sister Lady Jane Fellowes. Because their father, Robert Fellowes, is a royal equerry, they actually live within the portals at K.P., just across the courtyard from the little princes. On summer afternoons, the yard reverberates with noisy games and gales of laughter. There are rabbits hopping around in the garden, and the children love to play with them. During the summer, the Fellowes family also stays at Balmoral for at least a week—a great relief for Diana.

Diana's other sister, Lady Sarah McCorquodale, visits London three or four times a year with Emily Jane and George McCorquodale. But there is an even better opportunity for all the children to play together during what has become almost an annual event in the Spencer household. Diana's idea of utter paradise is to escape to a desert island with her mother, her sisters, and their children for a blissful beach vacation beneath the scorching sun. Airline owner and philanthropist Richard Branson obliged by making his remote island of Necker, in the Caribbean, available to these aristocratic vacationers. The Spencer women can sit around gossiping, catching up on lost time, knowing that their children are utterly safe.

William and Harry are a little too old to enjoy the company of Fergie's two daughters. In fact, William's first reaction upon hearing of the birth of Princess Beatrice was "Yuk, a girl!" Lately he seems to have changed his tune a little, discovering the allure of the opposite sex at a tender age, when Catherine Soames began to drop in at Kensington Palace for tea and sympathy with her two children, Flora and Harry. This was soon after Catherine had undergone a traumatic divorce from Prince Charles's good friend Nicholas Soames; Diana became a rock for her to lean on. Meanwhile, a romance burgeoned between Prince William and Flora, who frolicked around holding hands.

In many ways, Diana has succeeded in fulfilling what seemed an impossible dream: giving her boys a relatively average childhood. As Prince Charles puts it, "They are normal boys, growing up in abnormal circumstances." True, they get to stand next to their grandmother on the balcony of Buckingham Palace and wave at crowds of thousands of people, while watching an RAF flypast—but their idea of a *real* treat is to go for fish and chips or a plateful of sticky cakes at a café. To the astonishment of fellow day-trippers, Diana has also taken the boys to public amusement parks, standing on line with them like everyone else for rides on carousels and log flumes. (She's been photographed screaming with delight on the latter.) She resists any offers of red-carpet treatment or complimentary tickets, insisting on paying her party's entrance fees. With a smile in her eyes, Diana even paid a visit to the park's gift shop to pick up a badge that bore the legend "almost famous." Certainly, nobody could quite believe their eyes when Diana, returning William to school at Highgrove, dropped in with him at a Happy Eater burger bar, sipping on a calorie-free mineral water while Wills enthusiastically feasted on a burger, french fries, and ketchup, washed down with a large Coca-Cola. A burger king, indeed!

Diana's quest for normality has paid off. Prince William, once known as "His Royal Naughtiness," has now become a veritable Prince Charming. As previously mentioned, when Diana recently paid a surprise visit to London's homeless, spending more than an hour and a half talking to them about their plight and cheering them enormously, she revealed that it was William who had prompted her; he had become preoccupied by the realization that there were people who didn't have a roof over their head or food on their plate, and he pushed Diana to do something about it.

William and Harry's greatest asset is not their wealth or their privileged position; it is having such a caring mother. Only time will tell whether, as her children grow up and, inevitably, away from her, Diana decides to add to her family. When—on the same day and from opposite ends of Britain—Diana and Fergie *both* insisted that two children were enough and that they'd taken a joint vow not to expand their families further, they disappointed millions of royal-watchers who long for another baby to coo over and knit bootees for. Diana's father was saddened, too, and expressed his hope that Diana would change her mind about the two-babies-only pact. "I hope there will be more babies," he admitted. "It would be a pity if Diana did not have two more."

If Diana does decide to expand her brood—perhaps in the hope of regaining some of that early closeness with her husband, or just because she so clearly revels in the affection that her children (if not her husband) shower on her—she'll be keeping her fingers crossed for a girl. "I don't think I'd like to have three boys," she has said. "But I'd love a girl." One thing's for sure. It can clearly be seen from her great love of children—not just her own and her sisters', but far less privileged kids on whom she has lavished her time—that the Princess of Wales has enough TLC to go around.

# 9

# Charles — Prince of Wails?

*J*ust who *is* Prince Charles, the apparent "mystery man" that Diana fell for? This question puzzles the public, as they see the heir to the British throne stand on a soapbox and become impassioned about his favorite subjects: the environment; the horrors of modern architecture; the destruction of the rain forest; organic farming; Renaissance gardening . . . Indeed, the prince once described himself as "a thoroughgoing, organic crank." And as he disappears more and more often on seemingly eccentric jaunts—staying with a family of potato farmers on a remote Scottish isle, or packing his paintbox for yet another sketching holiday in the Italian hillsides—some have hinted that the prince himself isn't quite sure who he is.

Certainly, Charles is a man of contradictions. He will unflinchingly parachute from a plane, but admits to being "reduced to tears" every time he hears a favorite passage of music. But is he having an identity crisis? To suggest that would be to do the man a giant disservice. In fact, the prince on whom Diana set her heart as a teenager is in real life a charming, highly intelligent, well-read, and mostly humorous man—as those of us who've been lucky to chat with him can all testify. Some, in fact, would go so far as to say he's a visionary, who will one day make a great king—no mere figurehead, but a man who can inspire a nation.

He is a rich man (and potentially, upon his mother's death, one of the world's richest). But Charles feels that it isn't "done"—living opulently. His greatest pleasures come from the simple things, like growing his own vegetables. Highgrove is worth a comparatively modest $5 million. Technically, he is exempt from paying tax, but he chooses to pay 25 percent of his annual cash income (through the Duchy of Cornwall's property investments, which are technically his) to the Consolidated Fund, the equivalent of a state kitty. And if Diana thought that marrying Charles meant flexing her platinum AmEx and living like a jet-setter, she was in for a surprise: Charles, like his mom, is amazingly thrifty. His dressing gown, emblazoned with the Prince of Wales feathers, has been patched and mended. And Diana felt the lash of her husband's tongue when she bought him an expensive dinner jacket. "Money is such a vulgar subject," says Charles, reflecting a common royal view. It seems as if, like many millionaires, they continually think of themselves as hard up.

And it must be remembered that despite the riches, despite the antique-filled luxury in which he has been raised, H.R.H. Prince Charles Philip Arthur George has, almost his whole life long, been in an incredibly difficult position. Most eldest kids are under pressure to excel— but imagine how much worse that's made when you are born to a woman who will one day be queen and your entire destiny is mapped out for you from the day you're born. You may dream of being a train driver, an actor, a doctor, or an architect—but your destiny is to be a prince, with the strangest of job descriptions: shaking hands, making speeches, visiting foreign countries without being able to sneak off to the sights you yearn to see.

And, worst of all, there's the waiting. Charles knows that, as long as his mother lives, he's really a deputy—unless Elizabeth abdicates and thus allows him to take the throne during her lifetime. There have been whispers that, after forty years, the Queen might abdicate. But nobody really took much notice when, in answer to the question "how long have you been queen?" Charles's mama answered, "Far too long!" As Harold Brookes-Baker observes, "It's inconceivable. Since she took the coronation vows, promising to serve to the end of her days, I cannot imagine her breaking them. Her fellow royals would despise her. It's unbelievably important to them." So chances are Charles will only be able to take up his *real* job on what will undoubtedly be the saddest day of his life: the day his mother dies. And, with the royal family's history of impressive longevity, that might not happen till he's in his sixties.

When Charles was born, his grandfather, George VI, was still alive. George's daughter Elizabeth had begun life as a mere princess, who never expected to become queen. Her uncle, Edward VIII, George's brother, was set to reign over the United Kingdom. But Cupid had other plans. In 1936 he struck Edward with a thunderbolt: Wallis Simpson, an American on her second husband, arrived on the London social scene. Edward abdicated less than a year after he became king, handing over the monarchy to Princess Elizabeth's father. In 1952—Charles was just a small boy—his grandfather died of lung cancer while Elizabeth was on a tour of Kenya.

From early childhood, then, Charles has been groomed for the throne. Life has, naturally, set him apart from others; from the moment he realized he was different, he has also had to wonder whether those who sought to be his friends were interested in him or in being able to say that they were buddies with a prince. It's hardly surprising, then, that he confesses: "I'm happier with my family at home than anywhere else. We happen to be a very close-knit family." He can trust his blood relations in a way that he can trust nobody else, except the woman he chose for his wife.

As a small child, Charles was extraordinarily isolated. He took his lessons in Buckingham Palace with Princess Anne and a few other well-born children. Despite the fact that the Queen is one of the world's richest women, life was still fairly spartan: The heating in the palace is rarely turned up to a comfortable level. In addition, Charles would be left in his pram for a good chunk of the afternoon, even on the coldest days, to breathe fresh air in the palace gardens. Charles's father, Prince Philip, is well known for his ascetic habits—he loves cold showers, for instance—and believed that his sons should grow up to "be men," not cossetted and spoiled.

Charles's mother clearly loved him—and their relationship is still very close, very special. But duty called H.R.H. the Princess Elizabeth when her children were small, and she traveled far and wide, leaving Charles and Anne, two years younger, behind. Unlike Princess Diana, Elizabeth did not rebel against royal protocol and insist that her beloved offspring come along. So Charles grew up surrounded by courtiers, but with very few friends. And when he later went to boarding school—first Cheam Preparatory School, and then Gordonstoun—he'd had little practice at making pals.

Gordonstoun School, in a bleak, windswept setting near Scotland's Moray Firth, was Philip's choice for the "trainee king" (as his comedian friend Spike Milligan calls him); Philip had loved his time at the outdoorsy, macho school. But Charles is hardly likely to agree with the maxim that "school days are the happiest days of your life." He found himself almost friendless; he wasn't particularly good at the school's major sports—rugger, athletics, cricket; in fact, the only sport he's ever excelled at is polo, although Gordonstoun did leave him with a permanent taste for the outdoor life. And the other boys made it difficult for Charles; any boy who made friendly overtures was accused of brown-nosing. Academically, too, he was hardly the sort of pupil to grab straight A's. It took him three attempts to secure an "O" Level in math. And despite his fascination with history, he didn't shine there, either. On one famous occasion, his tutor apparently shouted at him in front of the entire class: "Come on, Charles, you can do better than this—after all, they're your family we're dealing with!"

Even though the teachers at Gordonstoun—perhaps out of diplomacy—picked Charles for "head of school," making him the highest-ranking pupil, the best time he had during the Gordonstoun years was actually abroad during an exchange visit to Timbertop School in the Australian outback. Miles from home, "mucking in" with the locals, Charles had a rare taste of what normal, everyday life is really like.

But at Gordonstoun, Charles discovered amateur dramatics, and loved every moment. He could shine onstage, and by playing a dramatic role, he could forget the burden of his *real-life* role. When he was chosen for the lead in *Macbeth*, the teacher who cast him declared him to be the finest Macbeth he had ever seen. And when Charles had to choose a university, he settled on Cambridge—not simply because it has a great teaching record and fabulous historic architecture, but because he knew that the university's amateur drama and comedy troupe, Footlights, might give him a chance to indulge this new passion. He got his wish, stealing the show in several Cambridge productions and proving himself as a comic talent. It's thought that Charles counseled younger brother Edward, who quit the ultra-tough British marines amid adverse publicity, to follow his heart into the world of theater. Much to their father's fury, Edward took a job as a gofer for Andrew Lloyd Webber, composer of *The Phantom of the Opera* and *Evita*. In fact, Edward may well have been living out Charles's own dreams.

Cambridge provided Charles with another diversion: the opposite sex. He'd had little exposure to women before that, having been isolated at an all-male school. But the press had already dubbed him "the world's most eligible bachelor"—and Charles soon discovered that one perk of being a prince was that there was no shortage of women just dying to date you. Despite being shy and gauche, he soon had a reputation as a ladies' man; perhaps he was following the advice of his beloved Uncle Dickie (Lord Mountbatten), who counseled: "I believe in a case like yours, a man should sow his wild oats and have as many affairs as he can before settling down."

The first girl linked with the prince was Lucia Santa Cruz, daughter of a former Chilean ambassador. She was never a serious contender in the long-term romance stakes, being Catholic and four years older than her admirer. She is now married to a Chilean politician and has four children; she and Charles still keep in touch. After Lucia, a long list of lovelies found a place in the prince's formerly lonely heart, among them Georgiana Russell, daughter of a former British ambassador to Madrid, and Fiona Watson, Lord Manton's daughter, who reputedly fell rapidly from favor when it was discovered she'd stripped for a girlie magazine. Charles's touching innocence was a thing of the past; as a child of the sixties, Charles enjoyed the freedom to become a man of the world. It was a significant transformation, in the eyes of fellow undergraduates, one of whom was quoted as saying, "When he first came up, he was astonishingly naïve about girls. He really thought that girls who slept with their boyfriends weren't 'nice.' "

You could never exactly say that Charles was wild— certainly not compared to the members of his generation who embraced the notion of free love. And the Royal Family have quite extraordinary double standards in the area of sex. As Uncle Dickie suggested, it's O.K. for a royal male to sow his wild oats—but when it comes to settling down, the Prince of Wales's bride *has* to be pure as the driven snow. Not surprisingly, this narrows the field of potential brides almost to zilch.

One who came close, however, was Camilla Shand, now Camilla Parker-Bowles. The two met after he had left Cambridge and settled on a career in the Royal Navy, following in the footsteps of his seafaring father. With a natural love of the sea, Charles rose rapidly through the ranks to command his own minesweeper, HMS *Bronnington,* where he was again to enjoy the experience of mixing with ordinary people, sharing cramped quarters with ordinary seamen from widely differing backgrounds. For one, with a warship's high-tech artillery to protect him, he was even allowed to forgo a minder!

Onshore, meanwhile, the romance with the vivacious Miss Shand was flourishing—indeed, she's said to be the only woman apart from Diana and Anna Wallace with whom Charles has truly fallen in love. It was finally the sea that separated them. Before a six-month stint on duty during 1973, Charles longed to ask Camilla to wait for him, but felt unable to. A month later, it was announced that she was to marry Charles's polo-playing friend Major Andrew Parker-Bowles. But they are still extremely close and regularly speak on the telephone; the Parker-Bowles's country home (where Diana is reputed to have lost her virginity) is close to Highgrove, and the couple are regular weekend visitors. Indeed, Camilla is, to this day, probably the truest, closest friend that the prince has—a fact that has sparked all sorts of rumors in the last few years about the true nature of their current relationship. Royal-watcher Andrew Morton maintains that Camilla even acts as hostess at some of Charles's Highgrove soirées—but if that's true, it's likely to be with the tacit approval of Diana, who is of the conviction that men and women can be just good friends.

Despite the failure of his romance with Camilla, Charles enjoyed his years at the helm of his ship. On and off duty, he developed a reputation as an action man (though he hates the label), parachuting, windsurfing, fishing, black-run and off-piste skiing, playing high-scoring polo, shooting, waterskiing, and generally acting the daredevil. As he himself has confessed, "I am a hopeless individual, because I happen to enjoy an element of danger. I think if you occasionally live dangerously, it helps you appreciate life." But as he moved toward his thirties, his naval contract was up, he had become a rounded, mature man—and it was time for H.R.H. the Prince of Wales to do more for his country than merely defend it at sea. But the role of monarch-in-waiting is ill defined. In the past, princes have been playboys. They've been mere puppets. But, with a deeply sensitive and caring side to his nature, Charles was determined to be *more* than that, realizing that he can do real good, helping to improve the lives of his loyal British subjects, before he ultimately gets to sit on the throne. He determined to establish what was wrong with his country—and do his damnedest to put it right.

He could, if he wanted, just sit back and watch his bank balance grow. Charles is one of the U.K.'s biggest real estate owners, with personal wealth conservatively estimated at $600 million (though he lags far behind his mother, who is allegedly a Six-Billion-Dollar Woman). But he is far more concerned about boosting the fortunes of others who weren't born so lucky. He has admitted that "I have a very well-developed conscience, I suppose, which is always needling me. I look around and I see so many people in far less fortunate positions than I am, and feel, 'Here am I in this position, what can I do to the best of my ability to improve their lot?'" One of Charles's greatest achievements is the Prince's Trust, a foundation that, among other functions, gives grants to ambitious young would-be businessmen and businesswomen to get their projects off the ground.

In order to raise massive amounts of money, Charles (encouraged, perhaps, by his music-loving wife) has harnessed the talent and enlisted the help of some of the world's most famous pop musicians, from Mark Knopfler of Dire Straits to Phil Collins, from Elton John to Eric Clapton—even though he doesn't even pretend to enjoy their music, preferring classical composers every time. The musicians donate album royalties and stage an annual fund-raiser concert. After one of these toe-tapping events—during which Charles himself could be seen laughing and jigging around in the royal box—he turned to one of the organizers and asked, "How much money are you going to make tonight?" "About £1,500,000, sir," he was told. Prince Charles let out his breath slowly. "I can't believe it," he whispered.

Over the years, the prince has become passionate about issues that—when he first expressed an interest in them—were often decidedly unfashionable. But time is proving that Prince Charles is no weirdo, he's just a little ahead of his time. Surrounding himself with a co-terie of expert advisers and confidants from all walks of life, who visit Kensington Palace and Highgrove regularly to keep the prince abreast of the latest developments in their spheres, Charles has his finger on the world's pulse. His great-uncle Lord Mountbatten once taught Charles to search for men with minds of their own, and Charles has ignored the civil servants, conventional thinkers, and sycophants. Only a generation ago, his mother followed a very different path; shielded from unconventional people, she was (and frequently still is) guided by courtiers, who are in turn advised by *other* courtiers. She is insulated from the real world.

But who makes up the court of her more worldly son? There are, of course, those rock stars—including Live Aid's organizer, Bob Geldof, who happens to be a friend of both the prince and me. (In fact, when I informed Prince Charles that we had Bob Geldof in common, he smiled and said, "Tell me this: Why doesn't he ever answer my letters?" "Well, sir," I suggested, not wanting to incriminate my friend, "he does get an *awful* lot of mail."

"Well, so do I," insisted Prince Charles. "Yes, sir—but he doesn't have an equerry to answer his!" "Good point," laughed the prince, who never minds a joke at his own expense). Geldof insists, in fact, in his autobiography, *Is That It?*, that "of all the people I met since 'Band Aid' began, Prince Charles is without doubt the one I have been most impressed by. I find myself more in agreement with him than anybody else. He is concerned, compassionate, highly intelligent—and, I think, nervous about expressing himself. He is a maverick and not just within the parameters of the royal family."

Prince Charles went "green" long before most Britons. He became increasingly concerned about the use of chemicals on his own farm—and so banned them, transforming Highgrove into an organic farm of which he is justly proud. He told me, for instance, that his wheat would soon be turned into flour for loaves of organic bread to be sold through the British supermarket chain Tesco's, where it was a sellout success. He declares, "I remain astonished at just how many other farmers still look at organic farming as some kind of dropout option for superannuated hippies. As one of those superannuated hippies, I have just taken the decision to farm the whole of the Highgrove Home Farm organically!" This will make Highgrove one of the largest organic farms in Britian. (Contrary to popular reports, however, Prince Charles is not a total vegetarian: His favorite meal is smoked salmon and scrambled eggs, followed by peach melba.)

Jonathan Porritt, former head of the conservationist group Friends of the Earth (and one of Charles's confidants), declares, "It wasn't quite so easy being green back in the seventies, so there aren't that many people around who have been genuinely committed to doing something about the environment over the past twenty years. Prince Charles is one of these, and it is this durability of concern that lends such an authority to his current environmental activities.

"Almost by definition," continues Porritt, "the prince finds himself in a world apart, yet his speeches on the environment never lose sight of the importance of personal responsibility, the need for individuals to help protect the environment through their own life-style. The lead he has taken on CFCs, aerosols, and organic farming has been carried out as much in practice as in eloquent declamation." Five years ago, Prince Charles was already recycling his newspapers, and many people thought he was weird. Now, millions are following his lead, and he's gained massive public respect. Charles says, "I've been talking about the environment for quite a long time, when I was just dismissed as a crank. Now I'm not going to *stop* talking about it."

Throughout history, the Royal Family has steered clear from discussing politically sensitive subjects in public—but the king-in-waiting has rewritten the rulebook. "I'm not stopping because it's become a political issue," he adds. "I'm going to go on even more now, because at least there's an audience! I've always believed in living life dangerously, to a certain extent—and this is just another aspect of doing so. And unless you actually get up and take up the fight, how are we ever going to get anywhere?" It is Charles's outspokenness that Diana has come to admire in her husband almost above any other trait. She knows he's not in the least crazy. In fact, he's one of the most sensible men she's ever known.

The prince detests the ugliness of much modern architecture, too, as his outburst on the proposed contemporary wing for London's National Gallery proved. A fan of classical buildings, he has even funded an architecture summer school in Rome, in the hope that the genius of Renaissance architects will inspire those who are to design and build Britain's future. He is unafraid to voice opinions from the heart; he ruffled politicians' feathers by protesting homelessness and asking, "Why can't the government spend more money?" He once denounced "the incessant menu of gratuitous violence" flooding our TV and cinemas. In the past, it was unheard-of for royals to be so outspoken. Their opinions might be aired at private dinner parties, but they always remained private until Prince Charles strode onto the scene.

But while Charles may be establishing a new blueprint for the monarchy, he cannot escape his destiny. At times, he tries—packing up and heading for the Tuscan hills to sketch, or spending a few days undercover on a remote Scottish island, joining in manual labor with the astonished farmhands. Charles has admitted that, at times, he feels like a prisoner. During an interview on CBS's current-affairs show "57th Street," with the glamorous anchorwoman Selina Scott, Charles referred to the torture of planning his every move six months, even a year, in advance. "That's for other people's convenience, because they want to plan *their* lives—their conferences, or their dinners, or their events, and I try terribly hard not to set my life in concrete, but that's what happens, regrettably." Selina then asked him if he felt trapped. "Oh yes. Oh, very much."

Charles's great escape from this regimented life-style was always to saddle up a polo pony and enjoy a few chukkas with his team, Les Diables Bleus, emerging soaked with sweat but with a big grin lighting up his tanned features. He might look at his diary at lunchtime, realize there was a break between engagements, get behind the wheel of his sleek blue Aston Martin, and be at the Guard's Polo Club at Windsor within half an hour. He reveled, too, in the relaxed social life that surrounds polo, one of the few realms where he can let his (thinning) hair down, jig about on the dance floor with a pretty girl, and have a few drinks. Some of these do's take place at the home of close polo-pal millionaire Galen Weston, who lives at Fort Belvedere, once the home of the Duke of Windsor. As Charles himself says, "I look forward to a game of polo more than anything else. I love the combination of horses, activity, and a team game. Polo is the only way I can survive in the summer, otherwise it would be a total nightmare. If I didn't get the exercise or have something to take my mind off things, I would go dotty."

And now a question mark hangs over that passionate pastime. Charles suffered a serious fall from his pony in the summer of 1990—and for a few moments, as the prince lay motionless on the sun-baked polo lawn, the nation held its breath in fear. He was lying still because he was winded—but he'd also suffered a fracture of his right arm, which to his intense frustration took months to heal. Spectators at the polo game recall seeing a bone "sticking out horribly at the elbow." When it wouldn't mend, he went into a Nottingham hospital for surgery to graft bone from his hip. His bulging diary for once remained firmly closed, with a pencil line through pages usually bursting with engagements at twenty-minute intervals. Diana had to stand in for him, taking on almost double her duties to fill the breach. In all, he was away from official duties for over four months—a time for serious navel-contemplation, and a quite extraordinary absence for a man who has been taught to put duty before everything else (even, at times, the needs of his family).

In fact, super-fit Charles became quite depressed at his inability to overcome the injury. He spent time in France, secluded from the world in a beautiful château with a pool, where he could exercise his arm—and he was photographed, by a paparazzo with a telephoto lens, staring forlornly out of the window. He passed the summer months on the banks of a Scottish river with his aristocratic nose in a good book, often separated from his wife and sons.

An amazing insight into the prince is given by the vivacious physiotherapist who helped put Charles on the path to recovery during that endless summer. "The one thing people never, ever realize about Charles is that he's absolutely delicious," she reveals. "From the point of view of a woman, he is a very attractive man. He really is. He is fantastic, sweet. He has all the qualities—compassion, sensitivity, morality. He is true to himself. A wonderful man."

It was partly the physiotherapist's care and encouragement that enabled Charles to overcome the terrible injury, taking up polo again the following summer. But doctors sought to put an end to his play when an old polo injury to his back flared up again. The prince, it transpires, has been in almost constant pain from a collapsed disc. (As one insider points out, "It certainly explains the fact that, at times, he can be very grumpy. There's nothing like back pain to torment you.")

Certainly, the Queen is thought to have had stern words about any plans Charles might have to play polo again. She believes it's too risky a sport for the heir to the throne—who just happens to be her beloved son—to indulge in. His polo fall was, in fact, his second brush with death in just three years: He narrowly escaped an Alpine avalanche that killed his close friend and staff member, Hugh Lindsay, and almost crippled another member of the royal off-piste skiing party, Patty Palmer-Tomlinson. Only the lightning reactions of the party's Swiss guide, who shouted, "Go, sir, go!" saved him.

Perhaps because he feared that polo was out of the picture, when Charles finally emerged from his convalescence he seemed muted, even bad-tempered at times. Perhaps it was that back injury flaring up. But Britain began to wonder what had happened to its Prince Charming. When reporters inquired about his health— he looked thinner, pale and drawn—he retorted, "What an original question! If you want to know, I'm barely alive." Many felt that the shock common to victims of severe accidents and falls had brought on a midlife crisis.

For alternative amusement, Charles has turned to gentler (although, to him, less satisfying) pursuits. He fishes, shoots, and paints; his dainty watercolors were received to great critical acclaim during a recent London exhibition. The prince has even tried his hand at the ancient practice of water divining! He has an enduring interest in "alternatives," from spiritualism (in an alleged attempt to contact his uncle Lord Mountbatten beyond the grave) to acupuncture. But this apparent eccentricity is simply an expression of the depth of Charles's insatiable curiosity; he is quite able to poke fun at himself on the subject of his esoteric interests. "I see things frequently saying I'm about to become a Buddhist monk, or live up a mountain, or only eat grass. I'm not quite as bad as that. Or *quite* as extreme."

Indeed, Charles's greatest passion (after polo) has proved to be one he shares with millions of his subjects: gardening. And that means getting dirt under his fingers, as well as planning his Highgrove landscape in great detail. I was lucky enough to be given a guided tour of the prince's exquisite, walled kitchen garden at Highgrove; he showed himself to be a great expert. It was as if he knew every plant by name. (And in fact, rumor has it that he *does* actually talk to them.)

He spoke fondly of the thriving herb garden, a wedding present from Britain's Women's Institute, "who kept ringing up and nagging, asking when they could deliver it!" Elsewhere, the prince beamed proudly at his peach trees. "My best crop yet," he smiled, leading a small group through the immaculately landscaped rows of every imaginable vegetable, interplanted with flowers; beautifully scented roses sprawled over pergolas. Incidentally, on that day, the prince could lay claim to a thriving greenfly population, too.

Highgrove's garden is a glorious place. Prince Charles is justifiably proud of it, even though he claims unfair advantage in being "the only chap to do his gardening by helicopter. And you know, I still can't get it right. We've put in a hedge that's going off at completely the wrong angle. Yet Lenôtre managed O.K., and jolly old Capability flipping Brown—and they didn't have helicopters!" He laughed at these references to great gardeners of history. Charles really is very funny, actually— and handsome, more so than pictures suggest. An interesting scar from an earlier polo fall runs down his cheek. But I have to say I wasn't too sure about the prince's clothes that day. Diana obviously hadn't been around to edit his outfit: blue shirt, gray suit, pink hankie, navy socks, and *brown* loafers—a combination that would certainly keep him off the best-dressed list.

Occasional lapses aside, Diana has smartened up Charles's sartorial act hugely. At her insistence, Charles's image has had a good spit and polish during the last few years. Lately his clothes, from his handmade John Lobb shoes upward, have, with their low-key but superb style, begun to attract as much attention as Diana's.

One inside story reveals just how much the prince has come to care about his clothes. Behind the sugar-pink palace walls in Monaco, panic reigned. It was seven forty-five and the future King of England was due to walk out into the balmy Riviera night to attend a gala concert in the palace courtyard. But Charles had no evening shirt, and neither the bull-necked Prince Rainier nor his skinny son Albert could come up with a plain white-lawn evening shirt, collar size fifteen and a half, sleeves extra long and double-cuffed to take Charles's Prince of Wales cufflinks. Queen Victoria could probably best have encapsulated his mood: "We are not amused." The valet who failed to pack the shirt is not likely to forget his night of shame.

Charles especially cares about his shirts. Although his wife is always coming home with high-fashion items—countrified tattersall checks from Ralph Lauren, pin-stripes from the Fulham shop Hackett, elegant Italian shirts from Bond Street boutiques—Charles is faithful in his fashion.

His shirts are made from his choice of fabrics ("some of them surprisingly jazzy," says a salesman) at Turnbull & Asser, on Bond Street. Their unique, cutaway collar shape was designed by him. "He has his own ideas, and he invented the collar shape more than fifteen years ago," says royal shirtmaker Paul Cuss. "The whole point of a bespoke shirt is that you can choose what shape you want as well as the basic material, and decide whether to have a stiff or soft collar."

Prince Charles usually goes for a luxurious Sea Island poplin ("It's a devil to iron," complains his staff), often in fancy stripes. The cloth samples are sent to Kensington Palace, where Diana helps Charles make a selection. She has also been known to pop into Turnbull & Asser's Jermyn Street branch after lunching at Le Caprice, around the corner.

Charles likes the crisp effect of a plain white collar above broad stripes. But the last thing he will choose is a stiff, starchy collar. "Have I absolutely got to? I loathe these things," he will say petulantly when dressing for a black-tie affair. In this he echoes his great-uncle, the Duke of Windsor, who was the first male to introduce a soft shirt and dinner jacket. (The duke also invented the "Windsor knot" for ties. Charles uses a Windsor knot today.)

"Times have changed," says Prince Charles wistfully, knowing it wouldn't do for a Prince of Wales to be known purely as a fashion plate these days. Only in his uniforms—over a hundred of them—can he play the peacock. "Uncle Dickie would have liked that," said Charles as he loaded on every possible decoration to attend Lord Mountbatten's funeral. The elegant earl designed the naval uniform trimmed with gold braid ("scrambled egg," to the royals) that Charles wore for his wedding.

The uniforms (which cost £1,000 a pop) are kept with their special shoes and boots, bagged up in plastic inside white hanging cupboards in K.P. During fitting for the uniforms, Charles comes face-to-face with his great-grandfather King George V. A dummy of the late monarch is used for uniform-fitting because Prince Charles's figure (particularly since Diana has encouraged him to eat less red meat and plenty of Highgrove green vegetables) is exactly the same shape as that of his royal ancestor. "His legs are longer," said the prince's former valet, Stephen Barry, "but the jackets fit perfectly."

For daily duty, though, Charles spurns this gold-encrusted splendor for a practical modern "uniform." And that is where Diana has really changed her man. First to go was his tailor. Now Charles uses Anderson & Sheppard, at 30 Savile Row, a gentlemanly establishment that also has a sprinkling of show-biz clients (the late Fred Astaire shopped there). The princess has banished Charles's overgrown-schoolboy suits in favor of double-breasted jackets and wide lapels, each with a dandified buttonhole (in which he likes to wear a rose, picked from the Highgrove garden). The trousers now mostly have cuffs, something ancestor George V would not have approved of. "Is it raining in here?" he once barked at his cuffed-trousered son, in the days when the cuff was meant strictly for muddy fields, not for the drawing room.

Diana has also been trying to change Charles underneath, buying snappy boxer shorts, with long legs like those of the swim trunks she found for him at Harrods on one of her early-morning visits to the Knightsbridge store on staff training day.

Charles does not go shopping; the shops come to him, or he sends one of his two valets out for him. "It's all done by the valets," complains a frustrated salesman, who feels that his shop's wide range of silk ties and pocket handkerchiefs is edited down to a sober selection by the household.

If there is one area where Charles could use some improvement, it is fatherhood. From spending almost all his time with Harry during the boy's first year, Charles has gone to the other extreme: He is all too often an absentee. The pattern was set before Charles's lengthy, contemplative convalescence, but as his sons grow up, the habit grows worse—and more puzzling. While Diana enjoys family outings to amusement parks or sporting events, Charles's rightful place is all too frequently taken by a private detective. When pictures appeared of Diana's yelling with joy on the exhilarating Thunder River Ride at Thorpe Park during a 1991 Eastertime outing with her sons, the question was asked: "Where's Prince Charles?" The surprising answer: He *hadn't* been detained elsewhere on official business. No, he was at a point-to-point race meet (an amateur cross-country race).

Lately, Charles seems to have been away from his sons more and more, pursuing sports or intellectual interests, and coming in for a lot of flak as a result. During a heart-stopping incident last year, Diana's and Charles's differing ideas of perfect parenthood became glaringly obvious. William was rushed to the hospital for a brain operation following some horseplay at his prep school: He got knocked on the head with a golf club and sustained a fractured skull.

"Operation Prince" (the palace's prearranged emergency plan) was put into action, and Diana, summoned by frantic detectives (probably upset as hell that they hadn't been keeping a closer watch on the future heir to the throne), was at the Royal Berkshire Hospital, where Wills was first taken, within minutes. Her husband joined her, but it was Diana who held William's hand during the ambulance dash to Great Ormond Street Hospital. A worried-looking Charles visited Wills there later; he discovered that an operation was necessary to right a depressed fracture of the forehead and eliminate the possibility that meningitis might enter the little boy's brain. But Daddy promptly upped and disappeared again, to meet politicians at the Royal Opera House for a performance of *Tosca*. Diana, meanwhile—briefly resuming her hated old habit of nail-biting—paced the corridor outside the operating room and stayed by her son's bedside to hold his hand and tell him everything was just fine when he came around from the anesthetic.

Unlike her husband, who hosted a panel discussion with a group of ecologists the following morning, Diana didn't resume her official duties until thirty-six hours later, when she was certain that William was going to make a full recovery. Although the strain on her face was obvious, Diana attended the opening of a hospital wing, managing a smile as she said, "Wills is all right now, but he's got a bit of a headache." With more than twenty stitches in his wound and with his blond hair shaved short for the operation, William left the hospital with Diana two days later. (Doctors say William should suffer no lasting ill effects from the mishap; but, as someone observed, "Think of the mental scars on the little boy who klonked him on the head and nearly killed the future king!")

It seems that at this stage in their lives, Charles has trouble relating to his sons. When William arrived home for his first half-semester holiday from boarding school, he raced happily into his father's study in London, only to find it empty—and he burst into tears. After a stern phone call from Diana to Balmoral, Charles faxed the boy a welcome-home letter.

He may have read endless books on psychology, and pored over Dr. Spock, when Wills and Harry were tiny bundles, but one simple fact may have eluded the prince: Growing boys thrive on a close relationship with their father, which facilitates their own passage into manhood.

But it is almost invariably Diana who is there with the loving touch, the demonstrations of warmth and closeness. Charles seems able only to look on admiringly at his wife's open affection. According to psychologist Jane Firbank, his apparent coldness probably isn't Charles's fault. After all, he was almost entirely deprived of close affection during his own childhood. Search back through the archives and you won't find one single picture of Elizabeth touching her son and heir when he was a kid. Says Firbank, "Emotional support is something Charles just doesn't understand or isn't able to provide. He can cope with the practical side of relationships, but he hasn't learned how to give reassurance and comfort. He is obviously a sensitive and compassionate man. Yet he just doesn't know how to translate that into a caring, personal relationship with his sons."

Prince Philip was reportedly also a distant and cool parent. He is also said to have been "somewhat despotic," forever pushing Charles into macho sports and feats of seamanship. This is thought to have been something of a trial to the young prince, who was by nature sensitive and artistic; perhaps he now means well, trying to take a backseat and let his own sons' personalities develop without interference. (And no doubt a trip to a theme park thronging with his subjects wasn't quite Charles's cup of tea.) Or perhaps he is biding his time, simply being a role model, waiting till his boisterous boys are old enough to share his pastimes before he bonds closely with them. But since he's so sensitive and forward-thinking in other areas, it is surprising that Charles doesn't follow the pattern of modern fatherhood and *share* with his kids more. Would it hurt to bite the bullet and ride the Big Dipper once in a while? There is a danger that if Charles waits *too* long to seek the closeness with William and Harry that Diana so obviously enjoys, he may never find it.

At least, however, the trainee king seems to have recovered a sense of purpose, even if that means taking on a punishing workload that keeps him from his loved ones much of the time. He has lofty ambitions, this man who refuses to remain a mere figurehead in a glittering coronet. And he is not going to wait around for his mother to abdicate, or for some terrible accident to befall her, before he gets on with the job of creating a better, more caring world. Certainly, this burning desire has earned him more than just the love and respect of his beautiful wife; an entire nation has fallen for his quirky, well-meaning ways, too. Many observers agree that Charles has the stuff of greatness in him.

Some even intimate that Charles honestly sees himself as a potential savior of the planet. He is planning to bring together influential figures from green charities, green politicians, and philosophers in June 1992 for a conference aboard the royal yacht *Britannia,* moored off the coast of Brazil, to try to work out a blueprint for preserving the planet. He clearly has great ambitions in that direction—but who can blame him? As one close friend once observed, "His mother's got the throne, and his wife's got the media. What's left for the guy?"

# 10

# For Better, for Worse

$\mathcal{I}$n fairy tales, princesses automatically live happily ever after. In real life, it takes a little more work. The young, naïve Diana spent so much of her engagement concentrating on the romantic side of her relationship, in frenzied anticipation of the day itself, that the reality of what life would be like after the celebration champagne went flat hadn't really troubled her at all.

Charles and Diana enjoyed a long honeymoon. After a magnificent wedding breakfast at Buckingham Palace, a wedding night spent in the blissful, bucolic surroundings of Broadlands House in Hampshire (where the Queen spent her wedding night, thirty-three years before), Diana and Charles made the most of a leisurely cruise on the royal yacht before joining his family at Balmoral for the traditional summer vacation. Diana floated around *Britannia*'s deck in a diaphanous negligée; she seemed, at times, to be flaunting her slender new body in front of the crew (who did their best to avert their eyes). At Balmoral, the pair were photographed holding hands and looking as much in love as newlyweds are supposed to be. At that summer's Highland Games—when Diana appeared wearing a stunning outfit in her husband's tartan—he was spotted tickling and teasing her. They appeared practically to swallow each other up with their eyes. The whole world went *"Aaah."*

Then, before Diana had time to settle into the routine of marriage, she had morning sickness to contend with; she had gotten pregnant during her honeymoon. It seemed impossible that Dianamania could escalate any further, but the announcement that Diana had fulfilled her vital duty as a baby machine escalated public interest even further. In fact, everything was turning out very differently from the way the couple had expected. Diana yearned for cozy domesticity but found herself in the wretched fishbowl instead.

Charles, meanwhile, had had his thunder stolen. He'd escaped his mother's shadow only to find himself standing in his wife's. He was naturally delighted that the public so approved of his choice, but perhaps he thought the adulation was going *too* far. When the pair split to greet assembled crowds on walkabouts, Charles found "his" throng staring over his shoulder, desperate for a glimpse of his wife. He should have been proud—but judging by his glum expression, he wasn't always. As one London cynic observed, "It seems to me that he's the only man in London not in love with her!"

Diana had probably hoped that marriage would mellow Charles, make him loosen up a little more. On more than one occasion, she's been overheard saying to her husband, "Oh, come on Charles, don't be so stuffy." But leopards don't change their spots—nor do thirty-three-year-old princes. A longtime loner, he found it very difficult to share feelings, not to mention living quarters. For the first few years of their marriage, there was constant minor squabbling as these two headstrong individuals learned to accommodate each other—and then make room for squalling babies, too. Prophetically, perhaps, Charles ruefully said to reporters before his marriage: "It's all right for you chaps. You can live with a girl before you marry her. But I can't. I've got to get it right from the word go."

In fact, Charles's domestic arrangements didn't easily admit Diana. He had his rituals, his staff, his hobbies, and his work diary booked up literally years ahead. Diana had to fit in wherever and whenever she could, so you can't blame her for the odd temper tantrum or rebellion. But still, the Royal Family was shocked to discover that the shy, demure young virgin quickly proved to have a mind of her own and wasn't averse to stamping her foot until things were done *her* way. (Perhaps if they had had a quiet word with Raine Spencer, they wouldn't have been surprised by Diana's headstrong ways. The new Countess Spencer once told Diana to go out and buy some "sensible clothes" for a memorial service, only to have her teenage stepdaughter defiantly acquire an outrageous outfit in garish colors.)

At first, Diana may well have resented the amount of time Charles insisted on spending with his family—but nowadays, she has learned to live with that quirk. When she was six months pregnant, staying at Sandringham, observers were aghast when a window flew open and a fair head appeared, as Prince Charles climbed into his Land Rover. "That's right, go and have lunch with your mother and leave me all alone!" yelled the princess, no doubt feeling fragile and frumpy, and jealous that she wasn't number one in her husband's eyes. She rushed out of the house after Charles, got into her car, and pursued him to the shoot he and his mother were attending. The startled beaters were astonished to see her rush over, face flushed, to her husband. "Why do you have to do this to me?" she hissed. "Why can't we just have a meal alone, for a change?"

This low point was counterbalanced by moments of great tenderness. Charles's loving concern for his wife was never more evident than a few days *after* this row, when Diana tripped and fell down the main staircase at Sandringham House. He ran to cradle her in his arms while they waited for a doctor to give Diana—and their unborn son—the all-clear.

But the differences between them became really obvious when the first flush of romance had ebbed. The basic truth had to be faced: Diana likes bubble gum, rock music, gossip, clothes, romance novels, and gentle sports like swimming and tennis. She likes giggling with girlfriends—and dancing with guys. By contrast, her husband is fascinated by architecture, history, and politics, by all-action sports like polo and shooting, by long philosophical discussions with his knowledgeable "gurus"—and by women he can *communicate* with. Observes a royal insider," When Charles says he's going to talk shop, it's Jung and community architecture. When Diana talks shop, she means Harvey Nichols." Diana simply isn't interested in most activities that involve deep thought; she thinks on her feet. This looks like a recipe for marital catastrophe—and for a while catastrophe was what this marriage seemed to be turning into. The two argued so much that a palace press secretary once found it necessary to warn a visitor: "If they start a barney in front of you, please pretend you don't notice."

Matters weren't helped when Diana suffered a dreadful bout of postnatal depression after Prince Harry's birth. She lost too much weight because she couldn't face food, and she became almost reclusive; the back stairs at Highgrove (which had long since been boarded up) were unblocked so that Diana could use them without running into her staff. She could hardly even look them in the face. It was a direct reaction against having to live the most public of lives.

There are thousands of T-shirts and needlepoint pillows that read, "When the going gets tough, the tough go shopping." That might have been Diana's motto; she seemed to buy her way out of her slump, shopping till she dropped in the Tiara Triangle. She was so regular a visitor to the shops along Kensington High Street that it was rechristened "Kensington Di Street." And none of this extravagance met with thrifty Charles's approval. He was already irritated because Diana's dazzling outfits, and even her hairstyles, claimed more column-inches than his carefully penned, heartfelt speeches. He felt his wife was becoming frivolous, behaving like a Hollywood superstar.

Diana had become lonely. Aside from Charles, she saw mostly his relations and the couple's staff. (There was friction there, too; in 1985, Diana decided it was time for her very own Changing of the Guard. She fired nearly forty longtime retainers and installed fresh, more modern-thinking replacements.) She could never have guessed how she'd miss the company of people her own age—and so she began, once again, to seek them out more often. Before her wedding, Diana had said to her roommates plaintively, "For God's sake, ring me up. I'm going to need you."

By 1985, she really meant it. She began spending more

time with the friends she'd made before her marriage; they were relaxed around her and didn't act overimpressed by her newfound status, which had begun to weigh heavy on her shoulders. And they introduced her to new people or reintroduced her to acquaintances. Exciting invitations began to wing Diana's way: to cocktail parties, bridge parties, and dinners (and above all, to her great delight, to go dancing, a pleasure that had been almost denied her since her wedding). Charles didn't try to keep her from her new circle of young, fun-loving friends; he didn't disapprove, at least not as long as *he* wasn't forced to spend time with them.

Their schedules began to diverge. Insisted Diana, "My husband and I get around six thousand invitations to visit different places every six months. We couldn't possibly get through many if we did them all together. So we have decided to accept as many as we can separately. This means we can get to twice as many places and twice as many people." But this explanation didn't quite wash, somehow. Even the Waleses' sons seemed no longer to provide that vital bond: From being an admirably hands-on father, Charles had begun to distance himself from Wills and Harry, too. Unlike other couples, though, who can sort out their differences behind closed doors, Diana and Charles had to contend with having every bit of body language, every cross word, every separation (however short) being scrutinized under a microscope by the press and public.

It wasn't long into the marriage before reports of dalliances on both sides began to trickle out. As early as 1986, the first rumor of an affair surfaced, the supposed duo being Charles and his old flame Lady Kanga Tryon. In fact, the delightful Kanga *is* close to the prince, and he's thought to have cried on her shoulder (figuratively speaking) when the marital path grew rocky. But Diana gets on extremely well with the attractive mother of four, who runs a flourishing dress-design business in smart Beauchamp Place; the pair have often lunched together at nearby San Lorenzo. The rumors of an affair were quickly quashed.

In 1987, Diana began frequently to be seen in the company of other men—handsome, aristocratic, dashing, *younger* men. She began to be escorted around town by Major David Waterhouse, "a childhood friend" and a nephew of the Duke of Marlborough. She seemed particularly to enjoy the company of Philip Dunne; she turned up at rock concerts with this handsome twenty-nine-year-old merchant banker, the Old Etonian son of the Lord Lieutenant of Hereford and Worcester. She was once photographed putting her head on his shoulder—an innocent enough gesture for an openly affectionate woman like Diana, but enough to spark rumors of infidelity that spread like wildfire.

A palace-watcher insists that "Diana's loves are all nonsexual." Nevertheless, eyebrows have been raised. For the great inequity in being a royal woman is that although it's taken for granted that princes and kings may have affairs, princesses (and queens) may not—especially if they're royal by marriage. Declares Harold Brooks-Baker, of *Burke's Peerage:* "Certainly, through history, the majority of men had mistresses. But George V, who was king during World War I, made the monarchy popular and created the aura of middle-class morality for the royal family. So, after that time, the men either did not have mistresses, or *pretended* not to have mistresses." Instead they shrouded their affairs in secrecy. But of course, in 1992, with telephoto lenses, phone taps, and gossip columnists everywhere, it is harder to keep these things private.

By the summer of 1987, however, things looked bad for the marriage. Diana publicly protested, "Just because I go out without my husband, that doesn't mean my marriage is on the rocks." Others weren't convinced, particularly after an unfortunate incident at the glamorous high-society wedding of the Marquess of Worcester and his aristocratic actress bride Tracy Ward. Prince Charles went home early from the wedding party—but Diana stayed on, dancing exuberantly with Philip Dunne till dawn. When a friend dared to ask if she had a lover, she laughed and said, "Yes, he's black and he's Catholic."

Then followed a lengthy separation over the late summer months. Charles, as usual, decamped to Balmoral, with his paints and his fishing rods—but without his wife, who stayed in London to kick up her heels with her circle of chums, using the excuse of a heavy workload. The Waleses weren't to spend a night under the same roof for over a month. The press, already excited over the state of the royal union, jumped at the chance to speculate about a rift. Diana and Charles, the darlings of the tabloid press, were vilified. Where once there had been an exemplary, happy family, there was now a deserting husband. Where once there was an adoring public, there was now a chorus of ugly innuendos about an affair (or affairs) and a marital crisis. FIGHT TO SAVE ROYAL MARRIAGE! read the headlines.

It was apparently at this time that the Queen put her foot down and told the couple to pull themselves together. Allegedly, her anger wasn't targeted at Diana at all—she told her son it was his responsibility to make sure that the couple's behavior was above reproach, to ensure that no shame or scandal be brought on the House of Windsor. "The Queen did not think that Diana had done anything wrong," insists an insider. But the couple were commanded to appear in public together. They did so, looking unhappy as they visited flood victims in Wales. But the purpose of that visit was almost obscured by the news that Charles had chosen to fly straight back to Balmoral rather than spend a single night with his wife at Kensington Palace. It was hardly a tactful, diplomatic gesture at a time of great stress, particularly since Charles had chosen to play host to two attractive (but married) women friends: Camilla Parker-Bowles and the outgoing Lady Sarah Keswick, a wealthy banker's wife who is the daughter of the Earl of Dalhousie.

An insider commented, "The palace flunkies can put forth as many excuses as they like. But the bottom line is that with no completely convincing reason the prince and princess are leading separate lives. It is clear that she is happier with her own set of friends in the south of England, while he is at his best living a rather spartan life in the north. What is worse is that the time apart doesn't seem to bother them. I think Charles has become totally bored with Diana, while she is just not interested in him physically."

Certainly, things seemed to have improved little when Charles returned to London during "the autumn of their discontent." At a polo game, he publicly exploded at Diana for sitting on the hood of his precious Aston Martin. It seemed that neither could do anything right. It was leaked, too, that at both Kensington Palace and Highgrove, the couple had separate bedrooms. But, as I've mentioned, there are practical reasons for this; by itself it's certainly no indication of a rift. Nowadays, though, they seem to require separate bedrooms more and more when on tour, even when their itineraries converge. Last year, in Prague, they were even separated by a cold, bleak stone staircase.

But it cannot have been easy for a stubborn woman like Diana to adjust to her husband's ways. "He really is a chauvinist to end them all," claims a pal of Diana's. "If he wants to go hunting, shooting, or fishing, he just does, and Diana has to fit in round him." It appears, in hindsight, as if Charles and Diana were simply testing each other during this long period of estrangement.

Nevertheless, it is really quite astonishing that during the summer of '87 the royal P.R. machine didn't immediately get on the case, encouraging Diana and Charles (at the Queen's behest) to present a unified front to the world. The marriage can't have been improved any by constant speculation that the pair were about to go their separate ways. But by late autumn, happily, things seemed to have been patched up again. Perhaps it took a while for the Queen's stern words to sink in, for Charles to realize that he was being selfish and that his duty was to be at Diana's side. He had a real obligation to talk through any problems, rather than escape them. And eventually, that penetrated his consciousness—and his conscience.

So on November 2, 1987, they were photographed in Berlin, radiating happiness at every turn, when the press had virtually been expecting the duo to arrive with lawyers in tow. Charles slid an arm around Diana's waist and pulled her gently to him while he whispered in her ear. Walking down a receiving line, the couple would normally have split up, but this time ignored the arrangement and stood together chatting to the wives and children of British servicemen. Everyone—

including, presumably, Her Majesty—breathed a huge sigh of relief.

In January, the couple took a second honeymoon, to Australia. And in three breathtaking minutes, the Prince and Princess of Wales revealed more about their marriage than a thousand press statements could. Dancing together (to Glenn Miller's version of "In the Mood") at a high-society ball in Melbourne—the first time in two years that they had danced before the cameras—they seemed more relaxed than ever. Seldom had so much happiness radiated from a couple so recently at the center of hurtful rumors about their marriage. They seemed lost in each other's arms.

Things may have been helped by Diana's growing interest in the marriage-counseling charity Relate. She took an increasing interest in their work; in turn, it heartened other troubled couples to know that even princesses don't always have magical marriages. Relate staff members have expressed amazement at Diana's insight into their clients' problems. "There is no doubt," remarked an observer, "that if she had the opportunity to counsel her future subjects, they would find her advice as constructive as any professional counselor's." In a recent speech on behalf of Relate, Diana declared, "marriage offers stability, and maybe that is why nearly seven thousand couples a week begin new family lives of their own." She could have been speaking from experience when she added: "Sadly for many, reality fails to live up to expectations. When that happens, most couples draw on new reserves of strength. But for many, their resources are not enough."

In fact, Diana's very varied work appears to have been her salvation. Charles had warned Diana that she wasn't marrying a man, she was marrying a job. But initially,

all the unworldly Lady Diana wanted was to be a wife and mother. She soon discovered that she was expected to be a "career princess," too. Fortunately, like many working women whose marriages aren't going too smoothly, she was able to throw herself into her career—and forget, albeit temporarily, about the ups and downs at home.

And since Disco Di was transformed into Caring Diana, there has been a marked improvement in the underlying quality and strength of her marriage. But that isn't enough to stop the rumors that occasionally surface at London dinner parties. There was talk, for instance, that Prince Charles had rekindled his affair with Camilla Parker-Bowles, that he had moved to Highgrove to be closer to her, and that he telephones her several times a day. This niece of Lord Ashcombe certainly does spend weekends in Scotland, evenings at Highgrove, and companionable afternoons on long hikes through the wildest countryside in Britain (just the kind of activity Diana seems to be allergic to). As a delicious postscript, gossip had it that Diana had been to Camilla's husband to plead, "Isn't there something we can do about this?"—only to be told that Princes of Wales had *always* behaved badly.

An insider says: "Charles and Camilla understand each other, they're the same stock, the same generation, and they love doing the same things. But don't imagine they're having an affair. They're almost too close for that. You have to remember that once their affair was over—and that was almost twenty years ago—Camilla took on a completely new role. She actually helped Charles choose his wife, giving the seal of approval to the young Lady Diana." But whatever Charles's rela-

tionship with Camilla, should any man spend so much time with a woman other than his wife?

Over the last few years, we've also heard Diana was madly in love with James Hewitt, the man who had taught her sons to ride. Another item of tittle-tattle had Diana engaging in a passionate affair with King Juan Carlos of Spain—which, everyone said, would explain why she liked to take her children for summer holidays with the King, and why Charles—the supposed cuckold in this regal triangle—always looked unhappy when he was forced to join them.

Whichever master or mistress of fiction ignited that rumor also raised a fascinating point. It is virtually impossible for Diana to have an affair. She has too much to lose: her homes, her position—above all, her sons. If the princess *were* ever to have an affair, her partner would have to be someone like King Juan Carlos, who would have just as much as she to lose if the affair were made public. Once the flames of passion had died down, a commoner, or even a nobleman, might be tempted to reveal the intimate details of a love affair with the Princess of Wales. Hell may have no fury like a woman scorned, but men have been known to be vengeful, too, and offers to kiss and sell would run into millons of dollars.

Even the logistics of an affair would prove impossible. Diana is trailed everywhere by a bodyguard, and the government must know her whereabouts at all times. Her servants are loyal to her—but they are loyal to Prince Charles, too. "While everyone looks the other way when royal men have their flings, it would be intolerable for royal women. Diana could have virtually any man in the world, simply because of who she is. But she won't."

Though nobody denies that Diana would win Olympic medals in flirting, that palace-watcher insists that "there is no doubt that Charles is the only lover that Diana has ever had and probably ever will have."

Nor will Charles and Diana ever divorce. The risks to the monarchy, in terms of controversy and public unhappiness, are too great for either to contemplate such a drastic step. He would have to ask his mother's permission, as Princess Margaret and Princess Anne did before their separations—and it's unlikely she'd give it. The Queen knows what a priceless asset the princess is to the "family firm," and how losing her might damage its reputation irrevocably. The contemporary image of royalty has taken many knocks; it might not survive the shock of this popular couple divorcing. Already, there are murmurings in Britain that the Royal Family is an expensive indulgence, funded by taxpayers' money. The Windsors wouldn't be the first European family to have the throne whisked out from under them.

Furthermore, when Charles is king, he will be head of the Church of England, which still frowns on divorce. Even in the unlikely event that the church sanctioned a divorce, Charles's position as its head would become completely untenable if he decided to remarry. (All divorcés have trouble finding an English parson who will agree to remarry them.) So the prince would be condemned to a lonely future, without a partner to lean on publicly or privately.

Probably the most emotional issue in the event of a separation, though, would be the future of William and Harry. Charles would undoubtedly claim that they are essential to the perpetuation of the monarchy, and must remain with him. Diana's chances of custody would be

less than zilch. And it's this, above all, that glues the Waleses' marriage together. Diana is utterly devoted to her sons and could not contemplate a future without them. She knows the agony her mother went through after leaving the earl and finding herself separated from her children as well. Diana could never bring that upon herself. When she was just a kid, she vowed it wouldn't happen. And she's sticking by that vow.

The reconciled couple do have their troubles. Charles is still occasionally jealous that Diana eclipses him on so many occasions. And it sometimes looks as if they haven't had a powwow lately about their diaries. On one occasion, Diana was making a major speech about AIDS, while Charles simultaneously lashed Britain's poor educational standards. One courtier reveals, "Charles was hopping mad over the clash of dates. He had spent weeks with one adviser, working on his education speech, writing and rewriting, only to discover that Diana was making a rare and important speech on the same day at almost exactly the same time."

Princes and princesses are no more likely to experience happy-ever-afters than the rest of us. The cheers, the flowers, the gilded coaches are a myth-building front for the fact that all marriages come, sooner or later, to the uncomfortable moment when two people look at each other in the cold light of day and realize they've married aliens. But after a roller-coaster decade together, Diana and Charles have established a working relationship, settling their differences somewhere en route. Aside from their two young sons, they do, after all, share a commitment to bringing a little light into the world, to improving the lives of their loyal subjects. It is a link between them that Diana and Charles share a

desire for a personal, human touch. And the harder Diana works, the more she has come to earn Charles's respect. She values no one's more.

During his midlife crisis, Charles may have questioned whether he'd married the right woman. But it's hard to see how he could have done any better. His difficulties with Diana are probably no different from the problems any long-established bachelor has in adjusting to a woman's presence. And if he'd been a commoner, could he ever have won the heart of someone so beautiful? So funny? So incredibly popular?

Certainly, while Diana grows more serene, Charles has grown more irritable with the years, as if waiting for the throne is testing his patience terribly. And, just like his irascible father's, Charles's temper always *was* terribly short; his former valet Stephen Barry once said, "None of the Windsors are worth speaking to in the morning. They are all bad-tempered and should not be approached before eleven A.M." (Perhaps those separate bedrooms may owe more to that single factor than anything else.)

"I have never been happier," Diana said recently. "He's the same man I married on my wedding day." She told a friend, "People jump to conclusions so easily. It is so easy to judge my marriage, but they don't understand me or my husband. I am never going to get divorced, and that's that. I am very happy, thank you very much."

It is certainly true that a woman who was miserable inside could never radiate the happiness that Diana does. And it's also true that Diana's husband hasn't changed; *she* has. But she now understands that Charles will always want time away from his commitments and his family, that he's a questing man who's rarely at peace with him-

self. The difference is that nowadays, she's strong enough to let him go when necessary, without feeling the need to draw attention to herself by shopping, disco-ing, or throwing tantrums. The days when she was jealous of his past, and his friends, have gone. Now, she simply accepts that he needs them.

The secret of happiness, in the Waleses' case, seems to be spending time apart. The adage "Absence makes the heart grow fonder" works for them. All couples lead separate lives, to some extent, and when you share a life under such intense public scrutiny a little air is almost a prerequisite of survival. Today, Diana knows that if she truly needed him, Prince Charles would be there. She is there when he needs *her,* too; when he broke his arm, she was a constant visitor at the hospital and made sure to drive her agonized husband home. She still occasionally leaves sweetly affectionate Post-It notes around for her husband to find. And in the privacy of home, it's still rare to hear the prince and princess call each other anything but darling. Romance's original flame, so apparent in the beginning, has mellowed into an enduring warmth. And occasionally, flashes of the old passion still spark between them, to everyone's relief, and most particularly to Diana's.

As the marriage vows said, it's "for better or worse." The Prince and Princess of Wales have had their fair share of good times and bad. But more than a decade on, they're definitely in it for the duration—destined, if not to live blissfully ever after, then at least, for most of the time, to live in relative contentment. Diana may have to weather her husband's bad moods, or resist the temptation of handsome men who long to seduce her. She may have to throw herself into her work, when once she

thought she would be reveling in a romantic marriage. She may often have to get her snuggles from two little princes, rather than one rather repressed middle-aged one. But whatever it takes, Diana, the crown princess, is going to do everything she can to ensure that she goes down in the history books as the perfect princess—*not* as the world's most famous divorcée.